REGIONAL AND RURAL DEVELOPMENT

Essays in Theory and Practice

Regional
&
Rural
Development

Essays in Theory and Practice

Edited by P. J. DRUDY

 ALPHA ACADEMIC

First published 1976 by Alpha Academic, a division of Science History Publications Ltd.
Halfpenny Furze, Mill Lane, Chalfont St Giles, Bucks HP8 4NR.

ISBN   0 905193 02 4

Printed in Great Britain

Contents

Preface   vii

1. Editorial Introduction   1
   P. J. DRUDY

2. Regional Development in East Anglia   11
   R. A. BIRD

3. Regional Development and the Attraction of Industry   23
   DAVID KEEBLE

4. The Role of Small Towns in Rural Regions   51
   MALCOLM J. MOSELEY

5. Rural Settlement Policy : Problems and Conflicts   59
   JOHN B. AYTON

6. Agencies for Rural Development in Scotland   69
   D. C. NICHOLLS

7. Development in Mid-Wales, 1957-73   91
   D. P. GARBETT-EDWARDS

8. Regional Planning Strategies in France   105
   I. B. THOMPSON

List of Contributors   117

Preface

This book arose out of a conference on 'Regional Development in Practice' held at Cambridge University under the auspices of the Regional Studies Association. The topic was considered to be of sufficient interest to be made available to a wider audience in book form. My sincere thanks are due to the contributors for re-drafting their papers for publication, to Professor D. R. Denman and David Wallace of the Department of Land Economy at Cambridge University and to my colleagues in the Regional Studies Association for their encouragement. I am indebted to the publishers for their guidance.

St Edmund's House,
Cambridge

P.J.D.

1. Editorial Introduction

P. J. DRUDY

There is now widespread recognition of the existence of regional inequality in advanced countries. Certain regions tend to lag behind the national average on such indices as income, employment, infrastructure and population growth. Over the last 40 years, governments have adopted a variety of regional measures in an attempt to reduce or eliminate these disparities. Yet today, in spite of significant economic progress at national levels, regional disparities still remain. In Britain for example, those regions which presently have the most acute problems are largely the same as those designated as *Special Areas* in 1934. The situation is similar throughout the developed countries of Europe and the United States; few nations can claim to have eliminated the inequalities and in some they have even widened.

Why has this been so in the face of an apparently impressive battery of regional aids and incentives adopted by many governments? There are a number of possible reasons. First of all, the objectives of regional policy have been insufficiently formulated and articulated. Secondly, some of the policy measures adopted, although well-intentioned, have been unsuitable for the achievement of the stated policy objectives. And some would argue, especially economists, that regional policy itself has been misguided and that the vast sums of money expended on it would have been better spent on other endeavours.

Looking first to the objectives, it is clear that regional policy may have a number of aims. These might include raising the level of income per worker or per head of the population, reducing the level of unemployment and out-migration, or improving the efficiency of industry. But just as at national level certain policy objectives such as full employment and price stability can be incompatible, certain regional objectives (for example, the maintenance of employment and industrial efficiency) could also

1

conflict. There is of course a potential conflict too between regional and national objectives. Thus, until such time as the objectives are clearly specified and given some 'weighting', it seems difficult to imagine how either regional planning or policy-making can take place with any significant measure of efficiency.

How suitable have the policy measures been in achieving their objectives? The answer will of course differ somewhat from country to country, but Britain is one area where the measures have been subjected to close scrutiny. It is therefore worthwhile to briefly review the record. Britain was one of the first nations to adopt serious measures at a regional level and since the 1930s successive governments have pursued some form of regional policy. Over the last three decades, both the 'stick' and the 'carrot' have been used in an attempt to reduce the inequality. The stick has mainly taken the form of a need to obtain an *industrial development certificate* and in recent times an *office development permit*. This 'control' system is designed to restrict any significant development outside the Assisted Areas, in favour of locations within them.

On the other hand, the carrot comprises a variety of financial inducements designed to attract employment to the poorer regions. These regions are now designated as either *Special Development Areas, Development Areas,* or *Intermediate Areas.* They cater for almost half the country's population and cover somewhat less than two thirds of its land area. The incentives include grants for plant, machinery and buildings, advance factories, low-interest loans, training facilities and a Regional Employment Premium.[1] In addition to this, government expenditure on infrastructure has been kept at a relatively high level in these areas. The measures adopted are thus quite impressive.

Two salient criticisms of the overall past approach to regional policy in Britain can however be mentioned. Firstly, the policy has almost always been dominated by a desire to reduce the level of unemployment. But it can be fairly argued that it was a misallocation of resources to adopt this 'social' orientation and to concentrate investment in areas of high unemployment, rather than at 'growth points' possessing good economic growth prospects. While the various regional measures adopted over the years were indeed designed to reduce unemployment, they were not in fact very successful.

A further feature of the policy, at least until recently, was the almost bewildering variety of changes in the various measures. Responsibility for the policy has also regularly been shifted from one Department to another as a result of administrative reorganisations. These constant changes, and the uncertainty they generated, could only have a deterring effect on any firm contemplating a move to the assisted regions. However, in recent years there have been hopeful signs that a longer-term approach is being adopted and the importance of maintaining continuity in incentives over a reasonable period of time in order to retain the confidence of industry has been accepted by the government.[2]

The 'growth point' idea was mentioned above. This notion, in various guises, has constantly recurred in the literature on regional planning and development over the past two decades and it receives some prominence in this book. The concept had of course been canvassed in Britain in the classic Barlow Report in 1940 and later in a White Paper in 1948,[3] but aroused little interest in those early years. It was only after the development of the concept of *pôle de croissance* by the French economist Perroux in 1955 that the idea began to be seriously examined in Britain and elsewhere.[4] Thus, in Britain the Local Employment Act of 1960, which concentrated aid on unemployment blackspots and largely ignored growth potential, was strongly attacked. Under this Act it would have been difficult, if not impossible, to pursue a growth area policy since places with good growth prospects were unlikely to have high unemployment. It was argued therefore that the policy should be replaced by one which selected areas with the greatest potential.[5] Such a policy could, it was suggested, alleviate the unemployment problem in the blackspots by short-distance commuting and migration.

To a certain extent this approach was adopted for two of the worst problem regions, with the publication in Autumn 1963 of White Papers on Central Scotland and North East England.[6] In Scotland eight 'growth areas' were selected, while a 'growth zone' was designated which covered much of the North East. Unfortunately, the criteria upon which the selection was made were open to serious criticism. In the main, political expediency appeared to have more weight than economic criteria in the selection process and a detailed analysis was carried out only in two of the Scottish areas.[7] In the North East, the area eligible for regional aid was simply extended so as to include some attractive as well as depressed locations, but a growth area policy was not pursued in any meaningful or effective sense. Nevertheless, the 1966 Industrial Development Act insured that incentives would no longer be concentrated only in areas of high unemployment. With the scheduling of *Development Areas*, incentives became available on a much broader basis and to a very large extent it could be claimed that the areas with growth potential were included.[8] However, it could be reasonably argued that the incentives were spread so widely over such a huge area of the country as to render them ineffective. This criticism is even more justified now since the areas eligible for assistance have been extended even further. Although 'growth point' and 'growth area' policies continue to be advocated for both the prosperous and poorer regions of Britain, their general adoption is still uncertain.

More serious attempts were made in France to implement Perroux's ideas and a number of *métropoles d'équilibre* were designated as counter-magnets to Paris. However, as Thompson points out in this volume, the idea has been now considerably modified in France also. Indeed, the very basis of the growth point idea – that significant 'spread effects' accrued to surrounding towns and rural areas – is being increasingly questioned.[9] It would appear that the evidence on the favourable impact of growth points is extremely scarce and the criteria on which they might be selected are still insufficiently researched or defined. If the concept is to be of any practical value, these knowledge gaps must be narrowed.

In relation to the effectiveness of British regional policy, one Committee put it as follows: 'There must be few areas of government expenditure in which so much is spent but so little is known about the success of the policy.'[10] Yet details on industrial mobility suggest that regional policy measures have had some success. Data from the Department of Industry (and Keeble presents some new information in this volume) point to a clear difference between 'active' and 'passive' periods of regional policy. During the active periods, significant industrial movement has taken place to the Assisted Areas while movement has dropped dramatically when the policy was pursued less seriously.[11]

Moore and Rhodes have attempted to identify the 'regional policy effect' in a number of useful studies. They estimate that between 1963 and 1970 regional policy had diverted about 220,000 jobs to the Development Areas. They further argue that the real costs of the policy in the 1960s were negative or close to zero and that, in terms of real disposable income, the benefits were enjoyed by all regions.[12]

A recent study by Buck and Atkins is however less optimistic about the effects of regional policy. These authors point to an apparently inferior performance of the policy for the period 1967-71 compared to 1963-67, even though expenditure had increased markedly.[13] But while there may not be total agreement on the exact magnitude of the regional policy effect, it is now widely agreed that it has brought some positive benefits to the poorer areas. Apart from the employment benefits mentioned above, there are also other strong economic arguments for a regional policy.[14] Perhaps the most important relates to the avoidance of inflationary tendencies. In the case of Britain it does appear that, due to a high level of demand, wage inflation tends to be initiated in the South East and West Midlands and then spreads to other regions. A reduction in factor demand in such fully-employed regions and its transfer to areas of labour surplus can thus reduce the rate of wage inflation.[15]

A crucial element in the evolution of adequate regional policies is the identification and analysis of problems in the different regions. In general terms the basic cause of regional inequality is the inter-regional difference in the demand for labour. In order to pinpoint the more specific causes it is convenient to identify three broad categories of region – the agricultural region, the industrial depressed region and the congested region.[16] Agricultural regions can be either of the 'marginal' or prosperous type, but in both types agriculture tends to be the dominant employer. In the marginal group, agriculture is usually in a relatively underdeveloped state. Physical conditions tend to be unfavourable, agricultural structure is poor, productivity and incomes are low and the out-movement of labour is therefore persistent. Obvious examples of marginal agricultural regions are found in Mid-Wales, the Highlands of Scotland, western Ireland, western France and southern Italy. In the prosperous agricultural group, significant productivity increases have occurred due to advances in mechanisation and improved techniques. Labour requirements have thus been reduced dramatically. In such areas there has been widespread redundancy and employment prospects in agriculture have declined.

The important point is that in all agricultural regions a consistent exodus from farming has taken place. This need not necessarily be undesirable since the agricultural industry is overmanned in many areas. However, a critical problem arises because the decline in agricultural employment is not usually counteracted by an expansion in alternative employment. Thus the vast majority of those leaving agriculture are forced to migrate. In addition to this the exodus has serious implications for the rest of the region's employed population, since a contraction in demand occurs in all sorts of services, resulting in unemployment and further migration. It is important for policy-makers to realise that these effects can be found in prosperous agricultural regions as well as in marginal ones.

Somewhat different problems are experienced in industrial depressed regions. These are areas which were industrialised and developed during the industrial revolution but which subsequently declined for a variety of reasons including changes in demand and world trade, different locational factors and a run-down of various resources. The problem here is one of economic re-conversion and development. Britain has striking examples of this type of region but many cases can also be pointed out in France, Belgium, Germany, Italy and the United States.

In congested regions growth rates and incomes tend to be high. Unemployment is low and there is a high inflow of new population. The main problems are the increasing social costs of congestion, the inflationary pressures and the decline of inner cities.

These various problems are closely inter-related and cannot be treated in isolation. A policy measure adopted in one region will inevitably have implications for another. It is evident therefore that there is a vital need for a close relationship between regional and national plans.

The topics outlined above are considered in more detail in the following chapters. In Chapter 2, R. A. Bird considers some important aspects of regional development with special reference to the East Anglian region of England. In the last few decades this region has experienced significant employment and population growth, and it has done so even though it lacked Assisted Area status and the accompanying incentives. It is well to remember therefore that factors other than direct government intervention can and do play a very important role in regional and rural development. For example, improvements in road and rail communications in recent times have certainly made mobility and 'linkages' much easier. Similarly, labour and space shortages, factory obsolescence and dissatisfaction with conditions in congested areas are also vital determinants of recent industrial mobility and regional change.

The attraction of new manufacturing industry to less prosperous regions has been a major element of regional policy in advanced countries. In Chapter 3, Keeble examines the pattern of mobility in Britain over the past thirty years and the main determinants of it. He suggests that a dramatic reversal of traditional industrial location trends has taken place, with preference now being given by expanding footloose industry to locations outside the older, congested industrial conurbations along the London–Lancashire axis. Keeble offers a cogent critique of the industrial complex approach to regional development and concludes that the 'linkage' requirements implied in this approach are in fact of little significance in industrial location. There is indeed impressive empirical evidence to show that the specialisation in particular manufacturing industries involved in industrial complex planning can be closely associated with below-average growth or even decline.[17] Because of recent trends in industrial mobility, Keeble further argues that total preoccupation with growth area concentration is unnecessary and probably undesirable.

The following two chapters, by Moseley and Ayton respectively, dwell on the desirability of selecting certain centres for development in largely rural regions. Moseley argues that an area's employment opportunities can be improved by concentrating public investment in certain towns and he suggests a number of criteria on which such a selection might be made. However, since the 'spread effects' of such towns can be limited, he calls for equally 'positive' policies for areas not chosen.

For some years, Norfolk County Planning Department has pursued a policy of selecting certain centres for development and, to some extent at least, accelerating decline in remaining centres.[18] The basis on which the selection is made in practice is examined in Ayton's paper. Studies carried out by the County Planning Department have attempted to identify critical 'threshold' populations which are required to support various services. Account is likewise taken of the existing and potential capacity of the various settlements and the cost of expanding them. The selection thus appears to be based to a large extent on economic criteria. But since adequate facilities and amenities can only be provided in a limited number of centres, Ayton argues that a concentration policy can be justified on social grounds also.

Development is unlikely to take place in the absence of adequate administrative structures at a regional and local level. Chapters 6 and 7 examine the role of several important bodies in rural regions. D. C. Nicholls provides a wide-ranging appraisal of the Scottish Highlands and Islands Development Board. In view of the success of this Board, he argues that the new Scottish regional authorities should have similar powers and financial discretion. Nicholls makes the crucial point that different regions have different problems and needs and that flexibility is thus vital. It seems inescapable that a relevant integrated land use policy can, in any case, be more adequately implemented at a regional level.

The Mid-Wales Industrial Development Association, described by Garbett-Edwards in Chapter 7, was formed in 1957 when the five county councils decided to cooperate in order to stem depopulation and to encourage development. The Association came into being due to the 'apparent disinterest and inaction by Government on the problems of rural Wales'. Garbett-Edwards examines the work of this body, the evolution of a growth town programme for the area and the particular experiment in development carried out at Newtown under the guidance of Mid-Wales Development Corporation. The contributions by Nicholls and Garbett-Edwards point towards the need for active regional development organisations with financial and executive power.

Regional planning and development in France is treated in the last chapter by I. B. Thompson. Like Britain, France has a wide variety of problems – congestion in the Paris region, industrial depression in the north-east and rural underdevelopment in the west and south-west. While a similar incentive and control system exists, a number of important differences can be identified in the French approach. For example, there has been an attempt to closely coordinate regional and national plans in a long-term perspective. Secondly, a considerable degree of executive power has been given to the Regional Councils which are composed of elected deputies and senators and elected members of local government. The development of a hierarchical system of growth points has also been an essential feature of the policy. Thompson provides a most useful critique of these and other measures in France.

While it is obviously impossible to cover all aspects of regional and rural development in one volume, these essays suggest that there is, at least, an emerging agreement on some of the most important issues. It is clear however that there is still a great need for a continuing identification and analysis of the problems, for a clarification of objectives and for a close monitoring of the success or otherwise of the ameliorative measures adopted.

REFERENCES

1. Although the Regional Employment Premium was to have been terminated in September 1974, it was in fact decided to continue it and to double the subsidy payable. See *Regional Development Incentives*, Government Observations on the Second Report of the Expenditure Committee, Cmnd. 6058, H.M.S.O., London 1975, p. 4. However, when going to press (December 1976), it had again been decided to abolish the Premium.

2. *Ibid.*, p. 11.

3. *Report of the Royal Commission on the Distribution of the Industrial Population* (Barlow Report), Cmd. 6153, H.M.S.O., London 1940, p. 223; *The Distribution of Industry*, Cmd. 7540, H.M.S.O., London 1948.

4. Perroux, F., 'Note sur la Notion de la Pôle de Croissance'. *Économie Appliquée*, Vol. 8, 1955.

5. See for example *Report of the Committee of Inquiry on the Scottish Economy* (Toothill Report), Scottish Council 1961.

6. *Central Scotland: A Programme for Development and Growth*, Cmnd. 2188, 1963; *The North-East: A Programme for Development and Growth*, Cmnd. 2206, 1963.

7. McCrone, G., *Regional Policy in Britain*, Allen and Unwin, London 1969, p. 211.

8. In addition, broader criteria for the selection of Development Areas were adopted, including not just unemployment but employment growth, population growth and migration.

9. See for example Hoover, Edgar M., 'Some Old and New Issues in Regional Development', in *Backward Areas in Advanced Countries*, edited by E. A. G. Robinson, Macmillan, London 1969, pp. 343-57; Moseley, M. J., 'The Impact of Growth Centres in Rural Regions: An Analysis of Spatial Flows in East Anglia'. *Regional Studies*, Vol. 7, No. 1, 1973, pp 77-94.

10. Expenditure Committee, *Public Money in the Private Sector*, House of Commons Paper No. 347, July 1972, p. 57.

11. Howard, R. S., *The Movement of Manufacturing Industry in the United Kingdom, 1945-1965*, Board of Trade, H.M.S.O., London 1968; Brown, A. J., *The Framework of Regional Economics in the United Kingdom*, Cambridge University Press 1972, p. 318.

12. Moore, B. C., and Rhodes, J., 'Evaluating the Effects of British Regional Economic Policy', *Economic Journal*, March 1973, pp. 87-110; 'The Effects of Regional Economic Policy in the United Kingdom' in *Regional Policy and Planning for Europe*, edited by Morgan Sant, Saxon House, Farnborough 1974, pp. 43-69.

13. Buck, T. W., and Atkins, M. H., 'The Impact of British Regional Policies on Employment Growth', *Oxford Economic Papers* (new series), Vol. 1, 1976, pp. 118-32.

14. A strong social and cultural case can also be made, but there appears to be less disagreement on this.

15. Brown, *op. cit.*, p. 331.

16. For other classifications see for example Allen, K. and Hermansen, T., *Regional Policy in EFTA: An Examination of the Growth Centre Idea*, Oliver and Boyd, Edinburgh 1968, pp. 47-53; Friedmann, J. R., *Regional Development Policy: A Case Study of Venezuela*, M.I.T. Press, Cambridge, Mass., 1966, pp. 39-44.

17. Keeble, D. E., and Hauser, D. P., 'Spatial Analysis of Manufacturing Growth in Outer South-East England, 1960-1967: Methods and Results', *Regional Studies*, Vol. 6, No. 1, 1972, pp. 11-36.

18. Norfolk County Council, *Interim Settlement Policy*, County Planning Department, Norwich 1974.

2. Regional Development in East Anglia

R. A. BIRD

Those people directly concerned with regional development and regional planning will know that the body of practical experience we possess is very small. Even more limited is the experience we can transfer with confidence from one location to another. It is urgent that we take every opportunity to evaluate each piece of working experience to speed up the evolution of regional planning. In this paper I wish to offer an over-all view of the past development of East Anglia and to relate this to some of the issues about regional development and planning that seem to require further thought.[1]

I have chosen to interpret my title by concentrating on the two words: regional development. My contribution is constructed around three qualities of these two words which I consider to be very significant. East Anglia I will use as a source of examples to illustrate these three qualities and the interplay between them. The first of the three qualities I wish to concentrate on is *ambiguity*: what is it we mean by the term regional development? The second quality is our tendency to regard regional development as a *good thing* to have – even if we are unable to define what kind of good thing we expect it to be. The third quality is our propensity to talk about regional development almost exclusively as a *spatial process* – and to disregard in practice many of the other significant processes which go to make it up.

The East Anglian background

To assist in illustrating these qualities, I need at this point to sketch in some of the important characteristics of East Anglia. First and foremost, it has the lowest population density of all of the English

11

regions. It reached this position by virtually standing still during the nineteenth century, while rapid population growth was taking place elsewhere in the country. The reasons for this standstill are not hard to uncover. East Anglia had none of the basic mineral or energy resources required for the industrial development of the period. Geographically it thrusts out into the North Sea towards the continent of Europe, so that when Britain adopted an Atlantic and worldwide role, its situation away from the main national routes minimised even the secondary ripple effects from the growth elsewhere in the country. The only significant development came in the holiday industry along the coast, and the agricultural depression of the late nineteenth century ensured that the main contribution of the region to the growth of the national economy was as a source of migratory labour.

The depressed state of East Anglia in the nineteenth century, and early years of this century, when there was no regional policy to alleviate it, is not without its compensations for the present day. Its legacy is that the region has retained a higher proportion of its historic character. Its towns and villages possess more of their form of the eighteenth century and earlier periods of prosperity than other regions. This not only gives a strong impetus towards conservation in planning policies, but is also a powerful force behind the rapid growth the region is now experiencing.

This reversal in the role of East Anglia took place in the 1930s, when it began to gain more population by inward migration than it lost by outward migration, and thus began to grow more quickly than the country as a whole. This change did not come about through any particular virtue of East Anglia, but rather as a result of an earlier structural change in the national economy, which returned to the southern half of the country the favourable position it had occupied prior to the nineteenth century. One reflection of this is that the same period saw the first moves in the development of regional policies at national level towards the depressed northerly regions – a preoccupation which is still with us today.

The Second World War ensured that Britain moved back to a primary concern with the continent of Europe – and the wartime airfields of East Anglia are mute testimony to this. Since the war the growth of East Anglia has gathered pace – it is at present running at more than double the national rate, and the prospects are that this rapid growth is likely to continue for the rest of the century. Indeed, the unique feature of the growth of East Anglia is that inward migration from other regions is more significant than the increase of its own population. Most of this migration is voluntary in that people choose to come there even against the incentives to locate elsewhere. Its origin is largely from the South-East region, and can be interpreted as the continuing outward spread of the influence of the London Metropolitan area. The most explicit form of this spread of influence is the planned migration programme expressed in Peterborough New Town and a number of town expansion schemes, mainly located in southern, western and central parts of the region. The planned migration programme is significant in a number of ways. Firstly, it is having a much more significant effect in altering the relative spatial distribution of the population than the numerically much larger voluntary migration which tends to adhere to established patterns. Secondly, it does not substitute for and reduce the level of voluntary migration, but rather acts as a stimulus for increased levels.

Looking inside East Anglia, we find that this rapid growth is taking place on a somewhat peculiar structure. The four main towns of the region, Norwich, Ipswich, Cambridge and Peterborough, rank at best in the third division of English towns, after London and the major conurbations. They are eccentrically located to the region, and communications between them are such that London is often regarded as the most convenient centre for representatives from all four towns to meet. As a result there are extensive rural areas which are still related mainly to a structure of market towns, whose functions are in a state of decline if not collapse. Perhaps the major source of this decline has been the postwar agricultural revolution, whose effects, while still largely undocumented, have been much more dramatic than, say, its predecessor, the enclosure movement. The official policy of encouraging the substitution of capital for labour has been very effective, particularly in arable farming in which East Anglia excels. The repercussions on the social and economic structure of the rural areas have been very large. There must be considerable regret that this has involved the severance of a strong cultural tradition of a close intimacy between the worker and the land, passed on over several generations. The urban image of the ruddy-faced countryman, placid and contented through his close contact with nature, has to be replaced by a countryside populated by machines, with crops sprayed from the air and factory farming for livestock. There must be some question whether the effects of such a severance are wholly beneficial. In a region like East Anglia, income levels still remain relatively low – and social security payments are less than grants to agriculture, and levels of car ownership are correspondingly high, with many workers dependent on their vehicle for travel to jobs in towns at some distance.

The process of regional development

I want now to return to the third quality I mentioned in the introduction – our general tendency to treat regional development as a spatial process, and to disregard the other processes which form part of it. I want to make this point, with reference to East Anglia, by looking at regional development as an investment process, carried out in complementary ways by the private and public sectors. Indeed, if regional development is anything more than a random process, it has to have an element of deliberate organisation, direction and support by the public sector. The first indicator we can examine is the degree of interest in East Anglia which is being taken by the private sector. Using the rate of private investment in new construction per head of population for this purpose, we find that East Anglia has the highest level of all regions and exceeds the rate of the next highest region, the East Midlands, by almost 20 per cent. This is confirmation that the prospects of East Anglia are very good. We find a very different picture when we examine the level of public sector involvement. The information that is available is not so clear-cut, but the evidence that exists suggests that public sector levels of both capital and current expenditure per head for East Anglia are close to or below the national average. Indeed, if once-and-for-all expenditures such as natural gas are extracted, then rates of capital expenditure by the public sector are lower than the national level. This tends to be confirmed when we look at local government expenditure alone, where a considerable level of dependence on central government finance through the support grant is evident. What this all adds up to therefore is that the public sector in East Anglia has been operating on a relatively low profile and not undertaking expenditure which falls outside the levels required to get by.

How can we explain this apparent anomaly that the expenditure of the public sector has not responded as yet to the rapid growth of the region as manifested in the expenditure of the private sector. It may be explained as a lag in the response of the public sector – and, as an extension of this, that the current phase is a transitional one before higher levels of public expenditure become necessary. There is some evidence to support this. A sizeable shift in the scale of resources given to road construction is taking place, largely as a result of the increased priority given to the A45 serving the expanding activity of the Haven Ports. The newly-established Regional Water Authority, despite efforts at pruning, seems to be faced with a much larger capital programme particularly on sewerage, and even so may have in effect to adjudicate on the location of new housing development in the next few years. It is significant that these two shifts are in basic infrastructure needed to support increased levels of activity. This indicates that, for a period since the war, the region has been able to absorb the growth it has been experiencing by drawing on its reserves or the slack in the capacity of its infrastructure. This is a process which can only go on for a certain period of time until those reserves are exhausted. If a prudent policy of adding to capacity has not been followed, what must result is a rather sudden rise in public expenditure, probably accompanied by a simultaneous check in the growth within the private sector. It is my estimation that this is what is currently happening in East Anglia, and that what we may see in the future is rapid growth achieved by jerks rather than as a steady process.

Let me recapitulate for you at this point what this means for any ideal view of regional development as a deliberate, thought-out process, and what it means for the agencies who are involved in it. What it suggests is that regional development on the part of the public sector is largely in response to the demands thrust upon it – and that these demands largely originate outside the region, rather than from some identifiable objectives or needs within the region which require to be satisfied. Consequently, those agencies which have a regional basis are forced into a reactive role in which their function is to struggle to keep pace with demands generated through the private sector. Only rarely, and probably only in marginal circumstances, is there a possibility of exerting positive discretion over the way in which those demands are manifested. The simplest means of making this point is to list the four agencies which currently possess the main impact on regional development in East Anglia. These are the Ministry of Agriculture, Fisheries and Food, the Greater London Council, the Regional Water Authority, and the private company responsible for the development of the port at Felixstowe – which is the mainspring of much of the present road investment programme. Not only does this list not correspond to the agencies which have formal responsibilities for regional development, but some doubt must exist on whether these bodies are fully equipped to cope with the implications of the roles they are forced to adopt in practice.

Why does this situation exist? Let us return to the nineteenth century and take some lessons from it. When the basic railway infrastructure of the country was created, it was through private capital on a risk basis. Today, we accept it as axiomatic that the public sector will take full responsibility for the provision of basic infrastructure of a similar nature. What I think we have to recognise, in regional development terms, is that the public sector is ill-equipped to undertake this role in a positive way. Its difficulties are legion. Resources are always scarce, and the venture capital it possesses is rarely given to projects of a regional dimension. It also has to contend with public accountability for the use of these resources, which builds in a disinclination to take risks. Increasingly, therefore, it has moved into devising routines for appraising suggested investment projects to demonstrate whether or not they are justified by the rate of return to the nation which they are likely to produce. These routines proceed by projecting demand, as generated by the private sector, usually on the basis of past experience, as such estimates of future demand have to be shown to be based on sound if conservative assumptions. As a result, those areas or regions which have only recently started to grow or whose rate of growth is rising will inevitably be under-represented in demand forecasts which may stretch over a ten-year horizon. Even more serious may be the way in which these routines tend to exclude from serious consideration any projects which are designed to stimulate rather than merely respond to growth in the private sector. Stimulated demand is something which is very difficult to include in soundly based forecasts of future demand, if the rules of the game are adhered to.

A second factor is that capital projects in the public sector are lumpy – they cannot be finely tuned to the exact level of projected demand. This has two important consequences in practice. Firstly, it tends to favour those areas where demands are concentrated – and can reach a level sufficient to warrant a step up in capacity. It is inevitable, therefore, that sizeable urban areas tend to benefit from this, and regions such as East Anglia with dispersed populations will have demands which themselves are dispersed. One result is that the provision of spare capacity in infrastructure, as a consequence of this lumpiness in public expenditure, will have the effect of stimulating further demand in the private sector, particularly when infrastructure capacity is in short supply. This leads to a process of cyclical reinforcement of growth in and around prosperous urban areas, and a gradual decline in activity in other less populated areas in a more static condition. In practice, this process, if I have diagnosed it correctly, has strong spatial implications. In East Anglia, it means that those areas in the south and west and around the main towns where growth pressures are already strong will be given further momentum by the process of public investment in infrastructure.

One final point in this picture of regional development as an investment process, is that regions with a low population density tend to have capital projects which are smaller than average in size. This is a very useful quality, in that it gives greater flexibility and scope to adapt over time to changing circumstances. But it also imposes a penalty that such smaller projects are much more susceptible to postponement in periods of national economic stress, and this is a situation which has been more frequent in recent years.

What I hope I have achieved by looking at the process of regional development in investment terms is to demonstrate that there are other dimensions to it than merely the spatial one, and that these dimensions may be more instructive in understanding what is taking place. The same point could have been made equally well if I had selected social or environmental processes for the same purpose. What I have not done either is to look at regional development as a political process involving choice – an arena in which the whole question of values and normative approaches would have to be considered.

The aims of regional development

What I want to do now is to consider the reasons why we tend to concentrate on the spatial process of regional development – beyond the obvious one that many of us began with a geographical training. I can do this by returning to the second quality I mentioned in my introduction – regional development as a good thing. This implies that public sector investment should be directed towards some positive purpose, presumably rather more than keeping pace with the demands generated by the private sector. It is not so easy to decide what these positive purposes are. Much of what I have said so far can be interpreted simply to suggest that East Anglia should receive a larger share of the national cake of public expenditure. This must imply a value-judgment requiring considerable caution. My own judgment on this question is that circumstances will ensure that East Anglia obtains a greater share. But I also know that every other region in the country is able to produce good and convincing reasons why their share should be increased. In simple terms, the generally favourable prospects which East Anglia possesses for the future do not suggest that on equity grounds between regions East Anglia has a wholly convincing case. If equity is to be our guide, the primary focus is internal to East Anglia itself, where it seems likely that future pattern of investment will widen existing disparities considerably – to the benefit of the urban population and the detriment of the rural population, and between the rapidly growing areas of the south and west and the less favoured centre, north and east.

It is in these circumstances that the spatial dimension of regional development becomes relevant, in so far as it acts as proxy for differential levels of opportunities and income. Compared to this, the routine of producing exact forecasts of the scale of population growth in the future, which will be wrong in the event, and then deciding on its most suitable location, is a sterile and not particularly rewarding exercise. In practice, the powers which are available to influence the location of population growth are marginal, and there are institutional difficulties in applying them consistently over any period of time. In effect, this influence is much smaller than the amount of uncertainty over the general scale of growth which will be experienced. The conclusion which I draw from this is that we have to try to be much clearer about the aims we are trying to achieve in regional development than we have been in the past.

There is one major and perhaps impossible obstacle in our way. The process of regional development is entangled within the working of a mixed economy, and so far we have no convincing theory of a mixed economy with which to work. In place of that, all that can be offered from current experience is a series of approximate guidelines, gathered and sifted from whatever experience exists.

The first of these guidelines rests on what I have already said about the place of a region in the national situation. We have to recognise that it is not practicable to regard a region as something which is isolated, and whose future can in some way be determined outside the framework of the national future. This can be illustrated more clearly in terms of the second guideline which recognises that regional development is a process of resource allocation designed to produce benefits. But the resources available for regional development are not solely those of the region. A considerable proportion of these resources come from the national level and are allocated to the region in the expectation of some form of a return to national welfare as a result. If we place these two guidelines together we find we are involved in the allocation of resources, coming from national and regional sources, to produce benefits both in terms of national welfare and for the population of the region itself. This can be approximated to a mathematical equation containing at least four elements, which means that there is no possibility of achieving an optimum or single solution, but rather a series of shifting balances between these elements.

One consequence of this is that we have to treat time as a separate dimension, and look at it as a profile rather than assume it away by fixing on an end-date for the form of development. We also have to distinguish and define each of the four elements I have referred to and break them down into their components so that the contribution of each component is placed in relation to all the others. This is not wholly straightforward, as I will demonstrate by looking at the benefits side of the equation.

So far our guidelines have identified two elements in the benefits we are looking for. The first of these I have called national welfare and this can be equated with the achievement of an adequate rate of return on the resources expended. In these terms, we have a body of theory in welfare economics and a set of techniques derived from that theory – centred on cost-benefit analysis – which make the attempt to provide a measure of this element. What is not present in this element is any consideration of equity or the distribution of benefits among the population. In my view, this resides firmly in the second element, where we are concerned with the population of the region itself. On a superficial basis we could treat this as equivalent to national welfare, and merely consider the allocation of resources which would maximise the regional rate of return. If we did this, we would merely have to add to our original equation the word 'local' which is at present subsumed in 'regional'. One reason why we are concerned with the benefits to the regional population is that we need assurance that the level of imbalance between regions is not growing too large. Equally therefore we need to be concerned with any imbalances within the region, to ensure that disparities internally do not become too massive.

On this basis it only requires a relatively small jump in the logic of the argument presented here to assert that the overwhelming concern of regional development with spatial processes is a not too well thought-out and imperfectly articulated concern with equity questions and how income is distributed among the population. Many of these questions only become evident in their spatial pattern. This linking of two of the qualities which I began with in the introduction must remain imperfect, however. We can have no clear-cut decision rule for regional or any other form of development which requires us to maximise equity, as this would require almost total regulation of every facet of people's lives to ensure that they received their exact share of the available goods.

How then can we begin in practice to put equity questions into some operational form? I think we can make a start by moving away from shares of goods in a concrete form, to the more abstract notion of opportunities – thus asserting some basis of equity in the exercise of choice, rather than what is chosen. In this way, we can identify opportunities as combining the activities which people can undertake, transport to move them to the physical locations of these activities, the income to pay for both the activities and the transport, and information or knowledge of what choices they can make. All we need to be able to do at this point is to find some way of measuring this!

A second approach is to re-introduce the time dimension. If we are sufficiently foolhardy as to be prepared to forecast what is likely to happen in the future, there are many instances where we can say with assurance that existing disparities will increase rather than decrease. I illustrated this earlier in drawing out the spatial implications of the investment process in East Anglia. We can hazard also that by applying the full extent of our powers to intervene in this dynamic process, it will be unlikely that we will be able to maintain even the level of disparities which we know today. In this situation, it seems to me that debate on the ideal or optimum level of equity to be aimed for is as academic and sterile in its content as trying to decide on the optimum size of towns. Even if we could find an answer, there is no realistic way of putting it into practice. All that is available to us under present conditions is to attempt to mitigate the effects of any potential growth in inequity.

One reason for this is the nature of the restraints we consciously impose on the use of public sector investment. I can illustrate this and round off my contribution by returning at last to the first quality of regional development which I referred to in my introduction – that of ambiguity. The word 'regional' is a perfect example of this in that of itself it has no precise meaning, and can only be defined by reference to what it is not. It stands for something which is more than local, and which is less than national. One result of this imprecision shows in the confusion over the way we use it. If I speak of regional policy, you will recognise that I am referring to that part of national policy which is primarily concerned with the distribution of industry between regions. If I speak of regional planning, you will immediately connect with the process of preparing a plan or strategy for a single region. What I want you to note is the antithesis in these between the words policy and planning. One of the words – policy – is concerned with what we are doing, while the other – planning – refers to a process of identifying policy choices and assessing them prior to putting one of them into action. What I cannot find is their equivalents. We have an absence of familiar terms to represent the planning stage prior to regional policy, and to represent the policy stage post regional planning.

What I think this illustrates is that we cannot be satisifed as yet that we have established firm policies at the single region level. Consequently, our efforts both in regional planning and regional development can be seen as attempting to restore some balance into our methods of allocating resources in the public sector. By building up a body of techniques, by constantly being critical and questioning what we are doing, by widening our approach to the other processes which contribute to regional development, we are constructing a body of experience and knowledge sifted from that experience which will allow the insertion into resource allocation of those objectives which are under-represented at present. Our attention to spatial processes, and the ambiguity which exists about what regional development is and what it is trying to achieve persuade me that the questions we are trying to come to grips with in this field are those of equity.

REFERENCE

1. The major issues for the future development of East Anglia are set out in *Strategic Choice for East Anglia*, Report of the Regional Strategy Team, H.M.S.O., London 1974.

3. Regional Development and the Attraction of Industry

DAVID KEEBLE

Ever since its inception with the 1934 Special Areas Act, United Kingdom regional development policy has been preoccupied with the problem of attracting mobile manufacturing industry from the traditionally prosperous regions of the South East and Midlands to relocate in the economically-lagging peripheral regions, such as Wales, Northern England, Scotland and Northern Ireland. This preoccupation with mobile manufacturing firms can of course be criticised on certain grounds. For one thing, national trends in demand and capital/labour substitution since the mid-1960s have resulted in substantial net *decline* in employment in nearly all manufacturing industries, growth being confined to certain service industries, notably finance, insurance and banking, and professional and miscellaneous services. For another, even within the manufacturing sector, greater emphasis is now rightly being placed on attempting to stimulate the growth of firms indigenous to the region, in the hope of developing a foundation of local enterprise and entrepreneurial skills which has traditionally been somewhat lacking in the problem regions.[1] But it is clear that, while policies designed to encourage indigenous manufacturing growth and the transfer of appropriate mobile service activity to the less prosperous regions are desirable, the attraction of mobile manufacturing firms remains very important for the continuing industrial regeneration of these areas. Moreover, as will be demonstrated later, industrial migration trends are also of considerable current significance for areas other than the United Kingdom's classic problem regions. Attention to recent trends and discussion of the industrial complex and growth area approaches to the attraction of mobile industry, the two main themes of this chapter, are therefore still very relevant from the viewpoint of United Kingdom regional economic policy in the 1970s.

Industrial mobility in the 1960s

Official Department of Industry statistics reveal that in terms of numbers of moves, industrial migration, defined here as the complete transfer of productive capacity to, or establishment of a branch factory in, a new location by an existing manufacturing firm, has been increasing in scale within the United Kingdom in recent years. This is clearly illustrated for movement at the broad inter-regional level by Table 1, which records the total national stock of manufacturing moves, and average annual movement rates, for four periods between 1945 and 1971. Movement here relates to the crossing of any of the boundaries separating the 11 standard regions into which the United Kingdom is divided for statistical and economic planning purposes. The figures thus exclude the considerable amount of short-distance movement which has occurred at the within-region scale during this period.

Table 1. Inter-regional manufacturing movement rates in the United Kingdom, 1945-71.

	Average annual inter-regional manuf. moves	Total U.K. manufacturing plants ('000)	Movement rate per 1000 U.K. plants
1945-51	142	98.6 (1948)★	1.44
1952-59	69	92.8 (1958)	0.74
1960-65	140	89.9 (1963)	1.56
1966-71	191	91.8 (1968)	2.08

Sources: published and unpublished Department of Industry manufacturing movement statistics: Abstract of Regional Statistics, 1973.

★*indicates estimate only.*

On the other hand, they do relate to *all* moves occurring during the period specified, whether or not the factories concerned are still operating. They also include factories established in the United Kingdom for the first time by foreign companies.

The table shows that the 1960s witnessed a substantially higher movement rate than that recorded for the late 1940s and 1950s, with a particularly significant increase from the 1950s onwards. By the 1966-71 period, nearly 200 manufacturing firms were establishing migrant plants each year in other regions of the

United Kingdom. At a more detailed geographical scale, with movement defined in terms of transfers or branches established across any one of the boundaries separating the 62 subregions used for official statistical purposes, no fewer than 1,786 moves were recorded by the Department of Industry during this most recent period, giving an average annual total of 298 migrant plants.

Unfortunately, this recent subregional migration figure cannot strictly be compared with data before 1966, since the Department of Industry substantially amended its subregional classification in that year. But on its old classification, which recognised a fairly large number of subregions (50) and a similar definition of all the main origin areas, inter-subregional movement between 1960 and 1965 involved only 1,404 moves, or 234 per annum.[2] So the evidence at this more detailed subregional level also suggests the possibility of an increase in the rate of manufacturing movement within the United Kingdom in recent years.

On the other hand, it is also true that although the number of moves has grown, the average size of establishment resulting from movement, measured by employment, appears to have fallen. Thus the 1,277 inter-subregional moves between 1960 and 1965 which were still operating at the end of 1966 were employing 229.6 thousand workers at that date, yielding an average size per move of 180 employees. This value is admittedly weighted by the atypically massive size of the Merseyside car assembly plants established as a result of government pressure in unique circumstances during the early years of this period.[3] But even if movement to Merseyside is excluded, the average size drops only to 160 workers per factory. This may be compared with a mid-1971 average for the 1,639 surviving 1966-71 moves of only 99 employees (162.0 thousand workers). Of course, allowance should be made for the fact that the measurement period allows an extra year for growth for the 1960-65 moves as compared with their 1966-71 counterparts: and that 1971 was in the trough, 1966 at the peak, of different national economic cycles. But even allowing for these differences, it seems probable that national trends in capital/labour substitution, possibly coupled with a greater willingness than before on the part of small firms to move to new locations, means that the average employment potential per move of recent migration is less than for earlier periods. *Total* eventual employment, though, given the larger number of recent moves, the shorter period allowed for growth, and the 1971 national economic recession, may well be very similar to that generated by 1960-65 moves, excluding vehicles.

The greater recent industrial mobility revealed by the above figures must reflect a variety of factors. One is probably the increase in speed and ease of road and rail communication within Britain over the last twenty years, which renders it easier for mobile firms to retain good links with existing customers, suppliers and so on despite movement. Thus, for example, the country's motorway network expanded from only 150 miles actually in use in 1962 to no less than 1,200 miles by 1975. In this connection, it could well be significant that Morley and Townroe's survey[4] of the main reasons for choice of a new location by moves to Northern England in the later 1960s found that accessibility/transport considerations were reported more frequently by the firms involved as an attracting factor than any other except government financial grants. The accessibility of northern locations was of course substantially improved by trunk road and motorway building programmes during that decade.

Another probable factor behind the higher recent mobility rate is intensified 'push' forces encouraging firms to transfer production away from particular origin areas. The nature of these forces has been considered at length in the literature.[5] But there is evidence that intensified labour shortages, resulting from rapid resident workforce decline, increasing problems of factory obsolescence, space shortages and cost, and growing psychological dissatisfaction on the part of industrialists and managerial staff with residential living conditions, are key factors behind, for example, the increased rate of movement from origin areas such as Greater London reported below (Table 2). In this connection, it could also be that the later 1960s and earlier 1970s witnessed a relatively new combination of circumstances encouraging increased migration not just of expanding firms, the traditionally dominant migration category,[6] but also of firms of marginal economic viability. As a tentative hypothesis, it might be suggested that the relatively difficult economic conditions of this recent period, coupled with the marked intensification in firm taxation via corporation tax, which was introduced in the mid-1960s, may have reduced the ability of a growing number of firms to finance continued operation and investment. In this situation, ownership of an increasingly valuable conurbation site might provide a substantial incentive for the firm to transfer production elsewhere to cheaper premises, the liquid capital released by sale of the former site being used for investment in new machinery and maintenance of production. The possible scale of financial resources released by such a move is illustrated by the much-publicised closure of the longstanding Rockware Group's glass factory at Greenford, in outer north-west London, in 1975 and transfer of production to factories elsewhere in the group, which involved, on informed estimates, the sale of the 140,000 square metre (35 acre) site for no less than £6 million.[7]

A third, and undoubtedly very important explanation for increased mobility is of course intensified government regional development policy. The 1950s was a period of only passive government action in this sphere, a fact clearly evident in the low between-region migration rate of Table 1. Since about 1963, however, Industrial Development Certificate controls on manufacturing growth in the South East and Midlands have been applied much more rigorously, while massive financial incentives have been made available to firms moving to the problem regions. For example, figures calculated by Moore and Rhodes[8] show that the annual average percentage South East/Midlands I.D.C. refusal rate, measured in terms of the employment involved, rose from only 12 per cent for the nine years 1954-62 inclusive to 21 per cent for the nine years 1963-71 inclusive. Moore and Rhodes[9] also estimate that the gross annual average cost of regional policy incentives to manufacturing industry setting up in the assisted areas rose from only £5.3 million in the 1950s, to £105.9 million in the 1960s, and £270.2 million in 1970-71: while a recent White Paper (Cmnd. 6393) gives actual expenditure in 1974-75 as no less than £441 million. The latter partly reflects the doubling of the Regional Employment Premium in July 1974. Though REP is now to be abolished, following the December 1976 public expenditure cuts, regional policy assistance will remain considerable. Aid is moreover now available, to greater or lesser degree, in a complex hierarchy of assisted areas – *Special Development, Development* and *Intermediate Areas* – which together contain over 40 per cent of the United Kingdom's population and cover more than 60 per cent of its land area. These facts suggest that the substantially-increased inter-regional migration rates for the 1960s, recorded in Table 1, are to a considerable extent a product of government policy.

The spatial pattern of industrial migration, 1966-71

The 1966-71 Department of Industry data also reveal that, in terms of spatial pattern, the main movement flows within the United Kingdom during this period again fit the so-called 'dual population hypothesis' put forward in earlier studies of manufacturing migration in Britain by the present author.[10] This hypothesis differentiates between short-distance 'overspill' movement from major industrial conurbations, generally within the traditionally prosperous central regions of the United Kingdom, and long-distance flows to the peripheral areas of higher unemployment. The former is further differentiated from the latter by a much higher proportion of transfers as opposed to branches, and a different and more growth-oriented industrial structure. Of total movement between 1966 and 1971, some 33 per cent, measured by employment created, fell clearly into the former intra-regional category, while 52 per cent involved long-distance between-region flows to the periphery. Interestingly, while the former is not significantly different from that calculated (31 per cent) for movement between 1945 and 1965 on the basis of the different set of subregions used by the Board of Trade before 1966, the latter is somewhat larger than its 1945-65 counterpart (46 per cent). So while increasing industrial mobility is evident at both the intra- and inter-regional scales, long-distance movement has nonetheless apparently grown at a faster rate than either short-distance overspill or non-categorised moves, almost certainly as a result of more active government regional policy.

Figure 1 maps 1966-71 movement, excluding moves from abroad, by employment created in the destination subregion by mid-1971. Of the ten areas receiving 5,000 or more mobile jobs during the period, seven – Northern Ireland, Glasgow, northern and southern industrial North East England, Merseyside, the South Wales valleys, and west South Wales – were in the peripheral regions. The three others – the Outer Metropolitan Area of South East England, Solent, and the central subregion of the West Midlands – were all reception areas for short-distance moves from central region conurbations. At the same time, however, many traditionally rural subregions also benefitted significantly from movement, examples including East Anglia, Devon and Cornwall, and rural Wales. Foreign moves (Figure 3: note that the symbol scale is substantially greater here than for

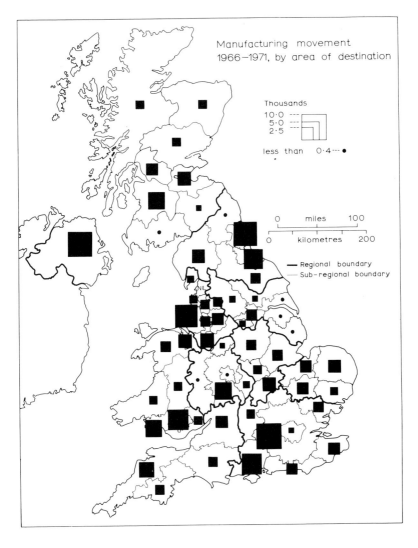

Figure 1

Figures 1 and 2) reveal a marked spatial bias towards the assisted peripheral areas (81 per cent of employment created), with an emphasis upon Northern Ireland and the Edinburgh subregion. Only 8 per cent of the employment created by foreign firms went to central subregions around London and Birmingham. This clearly illustrates the deliberate government policy of channelling new incoming foreign firms to the assisted areas, in marked contrast to the 'laissez-faire' trend of location of such industry around London in the 1920s and 1930s.[11]

The attraction of mobile industry has of course as the obverse of the coin the loss of this industry, both actual through complete transfers and implicit through growth foregone in emigrant branches, sustained by origin areas. Figure 2, with employment values mapped to the same scale as Figure 1, depicts job losses resulting from migration. Its single most striking feature is the relatively colossal loss of industry sustained by Greater London, manufacturing firms from which provided no less than 53 thousand jobs in branches and transfers set up in other areas of the country between 1966 and 1971. This represents 35 per cent of all employment created by inter-area manufacturing migration within the United Kingdom during the period. Moreover, as Table 2 shows, the 1966-71 loss reflects an increase in London's annual average emigration rate, calculated in terms of numbers of

Table 2. Manufacturing movement rates, Greater London, 1960-65 and 1966-71.

	1960-65	1966-71
Greater London factory stock, 1963 (1960-65 period) and 1968 (1966-71 period)	21,078	19,642
Manufacturing moves from Greater London surviving to 1966 (1960-65 moves) or 1971 (1966-71 moves)	511	550
Annual average movement rate per 100 London factories	4.0	4.7

Sources: published and unpublished Department of Industry movement statistics, and Abstract of Regional Statistics.

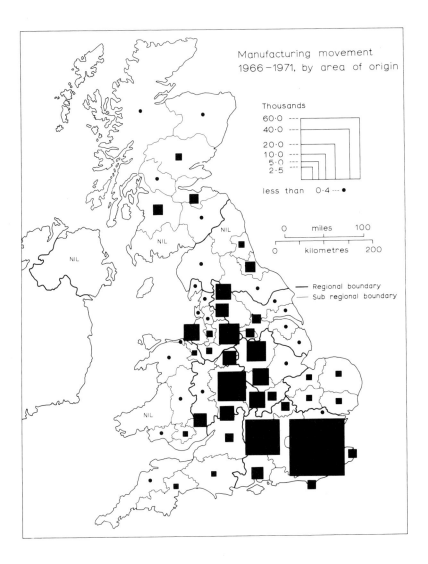

Manufacturing movement
1966–1971, by area of origin

Thousands
60·0 ---
40·0 ---
20·0 ---
10·0 ---
5·0 ---
2·5 ---

less than   0·4 --- •

Figure 2

moves and stock of factories in London, from 4.0 to 4.7 plants per 1,000 factories, 1960-65 to 1966-71. As suggested earlier, it is possible that this increase reflects in part a recent intensification of the forces acting to uproot metropolitan firms from their 'seed-bed' London locations. Not surprisingly, however, this uniquely high volume and rate[12] of out-migration is occasioning increasing concern and pressure from the G.L.C., the London boroughs, and London M.P.s for a modification if not reversal of traditional industrial decentralisation policy towards the metropolis.[13] This has recently achieved, for the first time since regional policy began over 40 years ago, reluctant central government acknowledgment of the case for slight moderation of development controls restricting small manufacturing firms already operating in the capital. This acknowledgment, made public in March 1975, has taken the form of a relaxation of I.D.C. control in Greater London only for manufacturing developments of between 5,000 and 10,000 square feet, such that developments of this scale when supported by the local planning authority will not normally be refused I.D.C. permission except on the personal decision of the Secretary of State for Industry. While unlikely to have any measurable impact in halting manufacturing decline and emigration from London, this first-ever concession could be very significant in the context of future government policy towards London, its industry and population.

A second major feature of the recent spatial pattern of migrant industry origins depicted in Figure 2 is the remarkable coincidence of losses with the traditional central 'axial industrial belt' of England running from London via the West Midlands to Manchester and West Yorkshire. Thus after London, the chief single origin areas for migrant firms were the Outer Metropolitan Area (a loss of 21,000 jobs) and the West Midlands conurbation (13,000 jobs), with Manchester contributing a further 7,000, Nottingham/Derby another 6,000, and Leicester, Coventry and Merseyside each another 4,000. Interestingly, the O.M.A. thus figures as both a leading destination and origin area, although its job losses from manufacturing emigration were nearly twice as big as its gains from inward movement, nearly all of which was from London. The whole axial belt, however, was of course the area singled out by commentators in the 1930s and since as Britain's major focus of industrial expansion and prosperity. The fact that it is now the country's major origin zone for mobile manufacturing

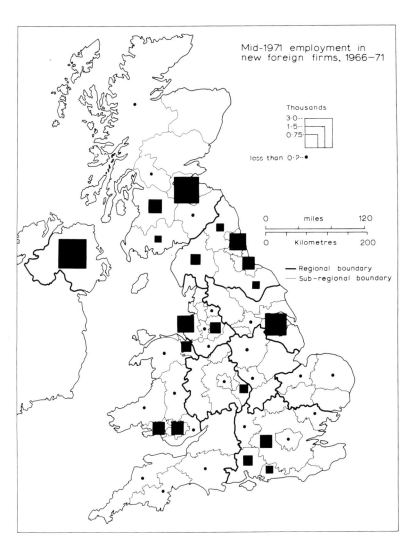

Figure 3

33

firms suggests a dramatic reversal of traditional industrial location trends, with preference now apparently being given by expanding footloose industry to locations outside the older, congested industrial conurbations along the London–Lancashire axis.

Changing regional industrial mobility rates, 1945-71

The last point leads naturally to the question of possible changes in regional attractiveness to mobile industry within Britain over the postwar period. One measure of such changes is the annual immigration rate of manufacturing plants, expressed in relation to the region's existing stock of manufacturing establishments. Unfortunately, the lack of co-incidence of official subregional boundaries for earlier and recent periods means that this calculation can in general only be carried out for inter-regional migration, although estimates for two important subregional destinations are also possible. A further important limitation is that the earliest date for which comprehensive Census of Production regional factory stock estimates are available is 1963, so that particular regional movement rates for the late 1940s and 1950s are likely to be less accurate than those for the 1960s.

Figure 4 however presents manufacturing movement rate trends, by destination and four postwar subperiods, for the two sets of central and peripheral/intermediate regions of the United Kingdom distinguished on the graph. As far as the latter are concerned, Wales stands out as the peripheral region consistently most attractive to migrant industry during the postwar period, measured against its total stock of manufacturing plants, with immigration rates of over 15 plants per 1,000 in both the 1945-51 and 1966-71 subperiods. Over the whole postwar period, Northern England ranks next with respect to high immigration rates, although Northern Ireland achieved a slightly higher rate during the 1950s and early 1960s. Scotland's performance was consistently the worst of the four peripheral regions. Both the two intermediate regions, North West England and Yorkshire and Humberside, attracted very little inter-regional immigration relative to their factory stock, although an increase in movement to Merseyside, North West England's chief assisted area, did raise the North West's rate somewhat during the 1960s.

These interesting trends suggest at least three possible

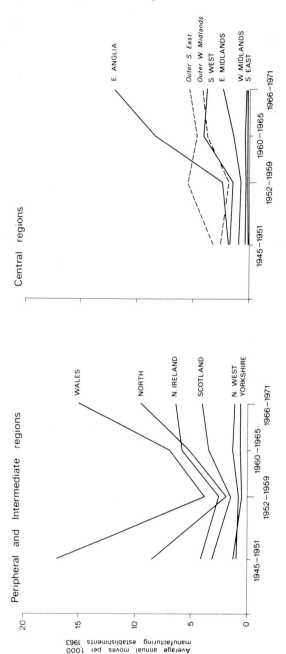

Figure 4

35

conclusions. First, assisted area status does seem to be positively associated with relatively high manufacturing immigration rates, as exemplified by the first four regions listed above. The existence of this 'regional policy effect' is moreover also suggested by the steep drop in all the assisted region immigration rates during the 1950s, an acknowledged period of weak regional policy. Second, however, the graph also suggests the existence of a 'distance effect' *within* the regional policy impact, in that the two most attractive assisted regions, Wales and Northern England, are precisely those closest to the central region conurbations in which most migrant industry originates. The performance of Wales, the nearest peripheral destination to South East England, the greatest single origin, is particularly striking. The third conclusion which may be drawn from Figure 4 is that leaving aside Britain's two traditionally most prosperous regions, the South East and West Midlands, the United Kingdom's least attractive destinations for inter-regional mobile industry throughout the postwar period have been the intermediate regions of the North West and Yorkshire and Humberside. This very poor showing adds further justification to the 1972 scheduling of the whole of these regions as intermediate areas, in need of an injection of mobile industry.

Although for convenience denoted 'central', the five remaining regions (Figure 4) include two, the South West and East Anglia, which are in fact relatively peripheral to the two dominant origins of manufacturing movement, the South East and West Midlands. The latter two regions naturally record exceedingly low immigration rates. But the right-hand graph of Figure 4 reveals that movement to the South West, East Midlands and, most striking of all, East Anglia, has in fact increased significantly over the postwar period. Indeed, by 1966-71, East Anglia's annual immigration rate (12.1 plants per 1000) was second only to that of Wales (15.1 plants per 1000). This very interesting finding again points directly to a marked distance effect in inter-regional migration, the most attractive destinations within the set of more central regions apparently being those hitherto non-industrialised areas which are located reasonably close to major origin conurbations. This is of course also suggested by the movement rates recorded in Figure 4 (broken lines) for the two part-region destinations of outer South East England (i.e. all of the South East outside London, including the O.M.A.) and the outer West Midlands (i.e. the West Midlands outside the conurbation). Taking the postwar period as a whole, immigration rates to the two key conurbation overspill areas have tended to increase, although the relatively very high 1952-59 rate recorded by the outer South East is an exception to this generalisation. The latter rate, which is in any case an underestimate because of the use of 1963 stock data, was in fact higher than that recorded by any region during the 1950s subperiod. But on the whole, and notably for the outer West Midlands, the graph suggests some increase in immigration rates through time, to a level about equal to Northern Ireland and Scotland by 1966-71.

In summary, then, the most attractive destination regions for mobile industry in Britain in recent years, measured by immigration rates, have been Wales, Northern England, and East Anglia. This grouping suggests the impact both of regional policy and distance from origin centres. Of secondary importance have been the peripheral regions of Northern Ireland and Scotland, and the somewhat more central reception areas of South West England, the outer South East and West Midlands, and the East Midlands. The North West and Yorkshire have been the least attractive of the set of possible destination areas, measured by immigration rates, at least up to 1971.

Movement as a component in regional manufacturing change, 1966-71

As a final aspect of this brief review of recent manufacturing movement in the United Kingdom, Figure 5 attempts to depict the short-term contribution of movement as a component in aggregate regional manufacturing employment trends between 1966 and 1971. The figures given therein differ from otherwise similar calculations presented for the 1953-66 period by Howard[14] in that while utilising the same sources – Department of Employment regional employment statistics and Department of Industry movement data – the latter are presented in terms of *net*, not gross, immigration. In other words, employment lost to a particular region by complete transfer of factories (but *not* branch plant establishment) elsewhere is subtracted from employment gained by that region as a result of immigration by both branches and transfers.[15] The resultant net migration employment estimate is given as the right hand column of the pair for each region in Figure 5.

In fact, even this net migration estimate undoubtedly underestimates the 'true' impact of migration upon most regions for at least two reasons. First, various studies show that migrant plants usually take a number of years to build up to full production and employment in the new location following movement. For example, analyses carried out in connection with work on the Strategic Plan for the South East[16] revealed that for a sample of migrant firms to various South East new towns, a period of very rapid expansion lasting usually four to six years was followed in a majority of cases by further growth at a slower rate for at least five years and often more. In general, then, most firms moving between 1966 and 1971 were very unlikely to have reached their full employment potential by as early a date as mid-1971. Equally, the apparently substantial growth of 'indigenous' industry, on top of net migration, suggested by Figure 5 for East Anglia and South West England, is probably largely due to the continuing expansion of firms immigrant to these regions *before* 1966 (see Figure 4).

The second reason for underestimation of the 'true' impact of net migration is that the measure adopted here assumes that only transfers, not branch plants, originating in a particular region such as South East England or the West Midlands involve actual job losses to that region. In fact, however, considerable evidence reveals that the establishment of branch factories elsewhere is very often followed by a reduction in workforce in the parent plant, with actual eventual closure of the latter in many cases. This process has recently been documented in detail by Atkins for 1966-71.[17] Her study shows that even for mature branches (i.e. those set up before 1961) employment decline by parent plants during the 1966-71 period was very substantial, and resulted from both complete closures and employment losses in existing plants. Parent factories of branches set up before 1961 thus recorded a net loss of no less than 143,100 jobs, or 17 per cent of their 1966 employment, between 1966 and 1971, 42,000 of these jobs being in complete closures. In contrast, their mature branches lost only 22,700 jobs, or 6 per cent of 1966 employment, largely as a result of closures (21,000 jobs). It is thus clear that the net migration declines recorded in Figure 5 for the country's two dominant origin regions, South East England and the West Midlands, probably substantially underestimate the true loss of manufacturing industry by emigration sustained by these areas during the period.

Despite these important qualifications, Figure 5 nonetheless

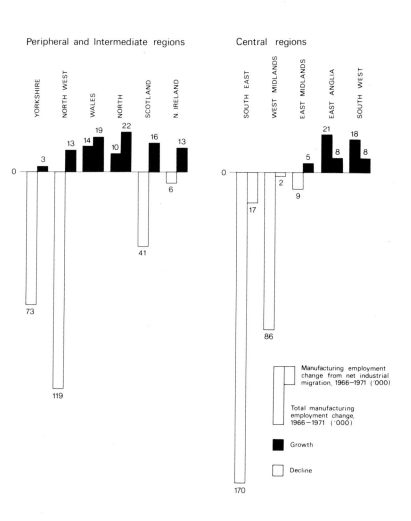

Figure 5

represents an interesting and hitherto unpublished analysis of the probable impact of inter-regional manufacturing migration upon recent aggregate regional manufacturing employment trends. In simple terms, it suggests that this impact varies in nature and extent between five distinctive groups of regions. Three of these groups encompass the peripheral and intermediate regions. The two latter, Yorkshire and Humberside and the North West, both recorded very substantial manufacturing employment decline during 1966-71, which was not offset to any significant degree by net manufacturing immigration. As noted above, this lends force to the argument that, in terms of manufacturing change at least, these regions are in genuine need of government regional policy assistance. In contrast, Wales and Northern England, a second group, recorded both aggregate manufacturing growth and substantial net migration gains. The latter in fact outweighed the former in both regions, indicating that without manufacturing movement, aggregate manufacturing employment in both these regions would in fact have declined over the period. The vital importance of such movement to the maintenance and growth of industry in these two regions is thus clear. Such movement was also of great importance to Scotland and Northern Ireland, the third group. But in these two cases, substantial decline of 'indigenous' industry, if that term can be used to encompass all manufacturing activity not involved in net migration as defined here, more than offset significant employment gains from migration. Without the latter, however, regional manufacturing employment would have declined much more than it did, particularly in the case of Northern Ireland.

The so-called central regions can be classified into two groups, with one region, the East Midlands, perhaps taking an intermediate position between them. The South East and West Midlands were characterised over this period by very substantial regional manufacturing employment decline, only a very small part of which appears to be attributable to net migration. However, the comments on this point made above do suggest that true net migration losses represent a significantly greater component of overall decline in these two regions than the figures recorded in Figure 5 indicate. This is supported by a very crude calculation utilising published figures in Howard[18] and Atkins.[19] From these, it can be estimated that by the end of 1966, South East firms which had established branch plants in the peripheral areas and adjacent regions such as East Anglia between 1952 and 1965 were probably still employing in South East parent factories just over 200,000 workers. This is estimated on the basis of a probable branch factory employment at that date of just over 80,000. Atkins, however, shows that employment in parent plants of development area and non-assisted area branches declined, 1966-71, by 16 per cent and 19 per cent respectively : and applying these percentages to the estimated 1966 South East parent factory employment yields a decline, 1966-71, of some 34,000 jobs. Of course, a decline of this order cannot simply and wholly be viewed as a direct consequence of migration, since national-level trends of declining manufacturing employment levels are also involved. But it does support the view that the 'true' net migration loss to the South East was probably at least double that resulting solely from transfers: and that migration is hence a more important component in the massive manufacturing employment decline of this region than Figure 5 suggests.

The other group of central regions comprises East Anglia and South West England, in both of which net immigration gains were an important component in overall manufacturing employment growth. Again, however, there are considerable grounds for arguing that the graph underestimates the impact, this time the positive impact, of net migration given the arguments presented above. This is probably particularly true of East Anglia, given the very high immigration rate experienced by this region since about 1960 (Figure 4). It is also noteworthy that this region, the smallest in manufacturing terms in the whole country, should have recorded a volume of aggregate but migration-led manufacturing employment growth greater than that of any other region of the United Kingdom.

In summary, then, while inter-regional migration is clearly of negligible or only moderate significance in recent aggregate manufacturing employment change in certain regions, notably Yorkshire, the North West, and to a lesser extent the South East and West Midlands, its importance for the maintenance and growth of manufacturing employment in a majority of cases, and notably Wales, Northern England, Northern Ireland, East Anglia and South West England, is very considerable indeed. This important conclusion thus supports the view that government regional policy, and within-region spatial planning, must continue to pay careful attention to manufacturing movement as a key component in regional and local economic change.

Industrial complex programming and the attraction of mobile industry

The two final sections of this chapter are concerned with the somewhat different question of intra-regional planning for industrial development within the less prosperous regions of the United Kingdom. In particular, they consider the desirability and feasibility of the so-called industrial complex and growth area approaches to location planning for mobile industry within these regions.

In recent years, certain commentators have argued that one desirable, if not optimal, approach to the problem of generating self-sustaining industrial growth in lagging regions is the planned creation of geographically-restricted linked industrial complexes. This idea owes much to the so-called growth pole theory of the French economist François Perroux[20] and his followers, although it also has independent origins in American work, notably by Walter Isard.[21] However, the specific application of Perroux's ideas to an actual region in the shape of a planned industrial complex was first recommended and worked out in detail by Tosco, in the E.E.C.-sponsored Italconsult plan for an industrial growth centre in the Bari–Taranto zone of that classic problem region, Southern Italy.[22] More recently, the concept has formed the basis of proposals by Economic Consultants Ltd for the industrial development of the Central Lancashire new town[23] and of an industrial growth centre in the New Brunswick maritime province of Canada.

These proposals are based on the view that one of the major problems of lagging regions, both in stimulating self-sustaining industrial growth and in attracting mobile industry, is the relative dearth of related supporting industries upon which key growth industries may depend for inputs and specialised services. Attempts to attract the latter, it is argued, will thus either be unsuccessful or, if successful, will have little multiplier impact upon the region in that most inputs will still be purchased by the incoming industry from elsewhere. Moreover, in the longer term, the extra transfer and other costs incurred as a result of these enforced long-distance linkages may render the activities of the new industry uneconomic. Protagonists of the industrial complex approach thus argue that the best policy for mobile industry attraction and the generation of self-sustaining growth is a selective one, involving identification of a suitable expanding and interlinked industry or set of industries. This is then followed by the simultaneous establishment within part of the lagging region of a carefully structured group of principal and subsidiary manufacturing units in this industry, such that the principal units benefit from the local availability of specialised and related inputs, while the subsidiary units are assured of major local outlets for their components or services. Clearly, scale factors are likely to be important here, since only a fairly substantial complex might be expected to generate sufficient demand for subsidiary and specialised inputs to warrant the establishment of units to produce these.[24] But the attractive apparent logic of this approach has certainly led such economists as Thirlwall to assert, specifically in the British regional development context, that 'the largescale development of growth centres containing industries which purchase from each other still offers the best solution for achieving regional balance'.[25]

It is however a fact that the industrial complex proposals for Southern Italy and Central Lancashire have either been unsuccessful, as in the former,[26] or rejected by government decision-makers, as in the latter; while the future of the New Brunswick plan appears to be in doubt. This clearly suggests that either in theory or in practice, industrial complex programming may not be as optimal an approach to lagging region industrial development as has been expected. In fact, at least three major objections can be raised to it, objections which probably explain its relative failure in the applications proposed.

First and foremost, much recent empirical evidence suggests that in contrast to what might be expected from industrial complex theory, few manufacturing firms in Britain and other developed economies appear to place great significance upon the local availability of linked firms. The corollary of this finding is that other factors are far more important in determining the locational behaviour of manufacturing firms, and in particular whether or not they will establish themselves in a lagging region. Three pieces of evidence may illustrate this point. First, the present author's 1963 study[27] of manufacturing industry in outer north-west London, a major natural twentieth-century growth centre, discovered that only 26 per cent of the 153 firms investigated reported any significant local input-output linkages within the area. Some 46 per cent recorded no local linkages whatever. Moreover, although it was true that firms in the area's key engineering and vehicle manufacturing industries were significantly more likely to exhibit local linkage than other firms, it was also true that what might be termed the 'linkage space' of these metal-fabricating firms extended over an area far wider than north-west London, embracing in particular the whole of the South East and Midlands of England. With certain specific exceptions, local 'within-complex' industrial linkage thus appeared to be of no very great importance as a location factor, a conclusion borne out by the fact that it has been the engineering industries which have spearheaded manufacturing movement *away* from north-west London in the postwar period.[28]

The second piece of evidence are the results of the Economic Development Committee for Motor Manufacturing's survey[29] of fourteen major British motor vehicle firms which established assembly (4) or component (10) plants in the Development Areas between 1960 and 1969. Although not specified in the report, several replies clearly relate to the post-1960 development of Merseyside as a large-scale motor vehicle assembly centre (see above). It can be argued that this development of principal assembly plants should, if industrial complex theory has validity, have encouraged the growth of linked industries in the area. Yet the E.D.C.M.M. survey found that 'although many component manufacturers in the sample had plant on Merseyside and in Scotland, only two stated that they had been attracted by proximity to vehicle assembly firms there'. Moreover, in answer to a specific question on the lack of supporting industries in the Development Areas, the survey discovered that 'perhaps surprisingly, only four firms had apparently been significantly influenced by this consideration', and that 'most firms did not regard such a factor as significant'.

The massive I.L.A.G. survey of over 500 mobile manufacturing firms which established plants across Department of Industry area boundaries (see Figure 1) between 1964 and 1967 provides a third source of evidence.[30] As with the other surveys listed above, this asked specific detailed questions on whether or not access to raw material or component suppliers, *or* a desire to minimise linkage disruption with existing suppliers, played any part in the firm's location decision. Again, the conclusion was clear. 'Distinctly fewer firms took supply forces into account than were influenced by the other factors so far reviewed'[31], only 15 per cent reporting supply considerations of any kind as a major influence upon their choice of new location. Significantly perhaps, the vehicle, electrical and instrument engineering, and mechanical engineering firms involved recorded even lower percentages than this (0, 11 and 14 per cent, respectively). This and the other evidence presented above clearly suggests that local linkages are not in fact viewed by most firms as of key importance for their activities, compared with other location factors, and that in a country as small as Britain, 'stretching' of linkages over considerable distances can occur without serious consequences in most cases. The first of these conclusions is also noted by Allen and Stevenson as a specific reason for the failure of the Tosco plan for Bari–Taranto.[32]

Two other important arguments against industrial complex programming concern its 'political' and long-term implications. First, it is fairly clear from what has happened to past proposals that establishment in a lagging region of an appropriate planned complex of particular industries is impossible in any other than a centrally-planned socialist society *without* a level of financial discrimination in favour of the area selected for the complex which is politically unacceptable to the representatives of other parts of the lagging region involved. Thus the fact that Economic Consultants were forced to propose special additional financial incentives for their Central Lancashire complex, *vis-à-vis* the remaining Development Area regions of Britain, in order to ensure the availability of appropriate industry, was almost certainly a major reason for government rejection. The long term implication argument against industrial complex planning stems from the very nature of this approach as *selective* of particular, specialised, industries, many of them dependent upon the few key principal units envisaged. This in effect thus represents a policy of industrial development through specialisation, in complete contrast to the traditional United Kingdom regional development policy of diversification.[33] The problem, however, with specialisation, as Perroux himself acknowledges, is that it is all too easy in the long run for growth to be replaced by decline. 'The concentrations of men and of fixed and definite capital accompanied by the inflexibility of the installations and of the structures which accompanied the initial development of the pole all make their

45

consequences felt once decline begins: the pole which used to be an area of prosperity and growth becomes a centre of stagnation'.[34] That this applies even at the local level has recently been documented by a statistical study of spatial variations in manufacturing change within outer South East England, probably the chief single conclusion of which was that manufacturing specialisation was significantly associated with below-average industrial growth or decline.[35] The long-term vulnerability of an intrinsically-specialised industrial complex thus represents another important argument against this approach.

Growth area planning

Industrial complex programming is thus very unlikely to be accepted as a feature of British regional development policy. However, the concentration for other reasons of mobile industrial development into relatively restricted parts of United Kingdom regions does appear to have received greater support in regional policy statements and from empirical studies. The 1963 Conservative government's attempts to institute 'growth area' strategies for industrial development in Central Scotland and North East England are well documented in the literature.[36] So also are some of the arguments for this approach, notably the lower cost of public infrastructure investment per head in larger rather than smaller urban-industrial centres, and the intrinsic logic of concentrating attention on those parts of lagging regions which possess the most obvious natural advantages – position, topography, and so on – for industrial expansion.[37]

More recently still, work for the Strategic Plan for the South East, which led directly to adoption by the Plan of a growth area strategy, has suggested that mobile firms are also likely to derive labour supply advantages from spatial industrial concentration.[38] This work, carried out by Economic Consultants Ltd, included a survey of the post-move labour recruitment experience of large (100+ employees) migrant manufacturing firms within South East England. Some 40 of the firms surveyed had selected a small town location (population less than 50,000), while 23 had established themselves in larger towns. However, some 45, 40 and 15 per cent of small town moves reported 'little', 'moderate' and 'severe' difficulty in post-move labour recruitment, respectively, whereas the corresponding percentages for large town moves were 65, 35 and 0. Admittedly, the relatively small size of this sample, and in particular the very low frequency of firms experiencing 'severe' difficulty, does mean that if one applies statistical tests such as chi-square for significance of the difference between these samples, which the Economic Consultants report does not, the results indicate that more data are needed before the apparent difference can be accepted as too great to have occurred simply by chance. But even in the absence of such data, the Economic Consultants survey does provide some support for the further 'growth-area' argument that larger industrial concentrations afford mobile firms an easier labour market situation than do smaller centres.

This all said, however, it would be unfortunate if the apparent logic and neatness of growth area or centre thinking were to blind planners and decision-makers to the empirically-observed fact that manufacturing industry is becoming steadily more dispersed, spatially, within Britain at all geographical scales, regional, sub-regional and local. This increasing spatial dispersion, to a substantial degree a result of manufacturing migration from large cities to smaller towns, and from urban to rural areas, has been clearly documented by several recent studies using techniques such as entropy index analysis. These include work by the present author on United Kingdom subregional manufacturing employment change in the 1960s[39] and by Martin on local area manufacturing employment changes within East Anglia, also during the 1960s.[40] Even more recent but unpublished East Anglian data show that the latter trend is continuing, with five of the region's six leading urban centres (Peterborough, Cambridge, Great Yarmouth, Norwich and Ipswich) recording manufacturing employment decline between 1969 and 1973, whereas 17 of the 20 remaining but much smaller employment areas recorded manufacturing growth, 11 of them of 25 per cent or more. These spatial dispersion findings are also supported by an earlier multivariate statistical study of industrial change in outer South East England, which identified a significant negative relationship for the early 1960s between settlement size and manufacturing growth, the latter indicating for whatever reason the apparent considerable attractiveness of small urban centres and rural areas to manufacturing firms.[41]

It can thus be argued that while growth centre or area strategies, such as that recently proposed for certain secondary settlements in

East Anglia,[12] have considerable utility, planning provision should certainly also be made for small-scale mobile industrial development in the more rural and less-urbanised parts of lagging and growing regions in the United Kingdom, and that such provision is likely to permit significant local industrial growth in many areas.

ACKNOWLEDGEMENT

I am greatly indebted to Mr R. S. Howard and Miss H. Gaskell of the Department of Industry for access to unpublished movement data, both for the 1945-65 and 1966-71 periods, without which this study would not have been possible.

REFERENCES

1. Keeble, D., *Industrial Location and Planning in the United Kingdom*, Methuen, London (1976), Section 4.1.6.
2. These figures differ from those given in Howard, R. S., *The Movement of Manufacturing Industry in the United Kingdom 1945-1965*, H.M.S.O. for the Board of Trade, London 1968, Appendix E, since they include an additional 97 moves, notably to locations in South East England, notified to the Economics and Statistics Division of the Department of Industry only after publication of the 1968 report.
3. Keeble, D., 'The Movement of Firms', Unit 8, 42 pp., in The Open University, *Regional Analysis and Development*, Course D342, The Open University Press, Milton Keynes 1974, p. 37; Riley, R. C., *Industrial Geography*, Chatto and Windus, London 1973, p. 189.
4. Morley, R., and Townroe, P. M., 'The Experience of Migrant Industrial Plants in the Northern Region', *Planning Outlook*, Vol. 15, 1974, p. 20.
5. Keeble, D., 'Industrial Decentralization and the Metropolis: The North-West London Case', *Transactions of the Institute of British Geographers*, Vol. 44, 1968, pp. 1-54. See also Keeble, *op. cit.*, 1974.
6. Keeble, D., 'Employment Mobility in Britain', in Chisholm, M., and Manners, G. (eds.), *Spatial Policy Problems of the British Economy*, Cambridge University Press, Cambridge 1971, pp. 26-29.
7. Keeble, *Industrial Location and Planning, op. cit.*, Section 6.5.
8. Moore, B., and Rhodes, J., 'Regional Economic Policy and the Movement of Manufacturing Firms to Development Areas', *Economica*, Vol. 43, 1976, Table A2.

9. Moore, B., and Rhodes, J., 'The Effects of Regional Economic Policy in the United Kingdom', Chapter 2, pp. 43-69, in M. Sant (ed.), *Regional Policy and Planning for Europe*, Saxon House, Farnborough 1974, pp. 61-2.

10. Keeble, 'Employment Mobility in Britain', *op. cit.*, pp. 42-53; Keeble, D., 'Industrial Movement and Regional Development in the United Kingdom', *Town Planning Review*, Vol. 43, No. 1, 1972, pp. 11-15; Keeble, 'The Movement of Firms', *op. cit.*, pp. 18-20.

11. Keeble, 'Industrial Movement and Regional Development', *op. cit.*, pp. 12-13.

12. For a brief comparison of rates of migration from London compared with other origin areas for the 1945-65 period, see Keeble, D., 'Industrial Mobility: In Which Industries has Plant Location Changed Most? – A Comment', *Regional Studies*, Vol. 9, No. 3, 1975, pp. 297-9.

13. Keeble, D., 'The South East and East Anglia', Chapters 2 and 3, pp. 71-152, in Manners, G., Keeble, D., Rodgers, B., and Warren, K., *Regional Development in Britain*, John Wiley, London 1972, pp. 94-7.

14. Howard, *op. cit.*, Table 2.

15. These particular figures also include employment in a small number of manufacturing plants set up by previously non-manufacturing organisations whose base of operations was in another region. Data on these have been collected by the Department of Industry only since 1966. Inclusion of these plants affects employment totals only, and slightly, in the cases of Wales, Scotland and Northern Ireland.

16. South East Joint Planning Team, *Strategic Plan for the South East: Studies Volume 1, Population and Employment*, H.M.S.O., London 1971, pp. 158-61.

17. Atkins, D. H. W., 'Employment Change in Branch and Parent Manufacturing Plants in the U.K.: 1966-71', *Trade and Industry*, August 30, 1973, pp. 437-9.

18. Howard, *op. cit.*, Tables 5 and 7.

19. Atkins, *op. cit.*, Table 3.

20. Perroux, F., 'Note on the Concept of "Growth Poles"', *Economie Appliquée*, 1955, translated and reprinted in D. L. McKee, R. D. Dean and W. H. Leahy (eds), *Regional Economics: Theory and Practice*, The Free Press, New York 1970, pp. 93-103.

21. Isard, W., and Vietorisz, T., 'Industrial Complex Analysis and Regional Development', *Papers and Proceedings of the Regional Science Association*, Vol. 1, 1955, pp. 227-47.

22. Newcombe, V. Z., 'Creating an Industrial Development Pole in Southern Italy', *Journal of the Town Planning Institute*, Vol. 55, No. 4, 1969, pp. 157-61; Allen, K. J., and MacLennan, M. C., *Regional Problems and Policies in Italy and France*, George Allen and Unwin, London 1970, pp. 318-27.

23. Economic Consultants Ltd, *Study for an Industrial Complex in Central Lancashire*, unpublished study for the Department of Economic Affairs, 1969; Livesey, F., 'Industrial Complexity and Regional Economic Development', *Town Planning Review*, Vol. 43, No. 3, 1972, pp. 225-42.

24. Allen, K. J., and Stevenson, A. A., *An Introduction to the Italian Economy*, Martin Robertson, London 1974, p. 205.

25. Quoted in Keeble, D., 'Regional Policy after Davies', *Area*, Vol. 4, No. 2, 1972, pp. 132-6.

26. Allen and Stevenson, *op. cit.*, p. 206.

27. Keeble, D., 'Local Industrial Linkage and Manufacturing Growth in Outer London', *Town Planning Review*, Vol. 40, No. 2, 1969, pp. 163-88.

28. Keeble, D., 'Industrial Decentralization and the Metropolis: The North-West London Case', *op. cit.*, pp. 13-17.

29. Economic Development Committee for Motor Manufacturing, *Regional Policy and the Motor Industry*, H.M.S.O. for N.E.D.O., London 1969.

30. Expenditure Committee (Trade and Industry Subcommittee), *Minutes of Evidence, Wednesday, 4th July 1973*, Session 1972-73, Memorandum submitted by the Department of Trade and Industry, Inquiry into Location Attitudes and Experience, H.M.S.O., London, pp. 525-683.

31. *Ibid.*, p. 589.

32. *Op. cit.*, p. 206.

33. McCrone, G., *Regional Policy in Britain*, George Allen and Unwin, London 1969, p. 215.

34. Perroux, *op. cit.*

35. Keeble, D., and Hauser, D. P., 'Spatial Analysis of Manufacturing Growth in Outer South-East England 1960-1967: 1. Hypotheses and Variables: 2. Method and Results', *Regional Studies*, Vol. 5, No. 4, 1971, pp. 229-61, Vol. 6, No. 1, 1972, pp. 11-36.

36. For example McCrone, *op. cit.*, pp. 210-11.

37. *Ibid.*, pp. 213-14; Allen, K. J., and Hermansen, T., *Regional Policy in EFTA: An Examination of the Growth Centre Idea*, Oliver and Boyd, Edinburgh 1968, pp. 73-108.

38. South East Joint Planning Team, *Strategic Plan for the South East: Studies Volume 5, Report of Economic Consultants Ltd.*, H.M.S.O., London 1971, p. 76.

39. Keeble, *Industrial Location and Planning, op. cit.*, Section 2.3.

40. Martin, R. L., *Information Theory and Employment Location Trends in East Anglia*, Department of Geography, Cambridge University 1972.

41. Keeble and Hauser, *op. cit.*, 1972, p. 30.

42. East Anglia Regional Strategy Team, *Strategic Choice for East Anglia*, H.M.S.O., London 1974, p. 66.

4. The Role of Small Towns in Rural Regions

MALCOLM J. MOSELEY

Three themes that are discernible in the recent history of regional planning set a context for what I want to discuss in this chapter. First, the word 'development' in the conference title makes me think that five or ten years ago our topic might perhaps have been 'regional *growth* in practice'. But today our focus is 'development' which I take to relate to the transformation of social and economic systems, not just the expansion of their constituent parts, and transformation moreover in the direction of predetermined objectives. A second theme relates to the moving together of urban policies and regional policies: towns are increasingly seen as agencies of regional development. In 1955 Lampard asked whether cities have in some way acted as a force for socio-economic change[1] – a question which now seems rather trite. Scottish new towns, for example, have been conceived not just as receptacles for overspill but as agencies in the creation of an environment in Central Scotland much more conducive to regional development. The third interesting shift that I want to mention relates to the movement away from objectives of 'place prosperity', towards those of 'people prosperity'. Hoover, for example, has suggested that the only legitimate aim of public policy is to improve the welfare of *people* rather than of *areas* as such.[2] This means that if new employment opportunities are not so mobile as to make possible their dispersal to every 'problem area', and if people in 'problem areas' are not themselves totally immobile, then in order best to realise their wants and needs it may be advisable *not* to attempt to shift employment opportunities all the way to their present places of residence. Such an argument points instead to the merits of a 'compromise' policy, in which both employment opportunities and labour move some way towards the other.

These three themes provide a context for a consideration of the

51

potential role of small towns in rural regions. My definitions of 'small towns' and 'rural regions' are not particulary rigorous. I shall be talking essentially of towns in the 2,000–20,000 population size range, and of those parts of the country which lie beyond the immediate commuting hinterland of towns with at least about 50,000 inhabitants: rough and arbitrary definitions. And I shall be looking at small towns in a planning context, that is looking at their possible role in a settlement hierarchy devised to meet certain predefined objectives. I should perhaps stress the word hierarchy, and say at the outset that I find little value in notions of a single optimum city size. Different towns have different roles to perform. Clearly it is absurd to imagine that every town should contain, say, a hospital: just as absurd in fact as imagining that *no* towns should have such a facility. The goal must be one of devising an urban system best able to meet a set of objectives.

Problems in rural areas

Objective specification should presumably follow from an identification of problems. A great deal has been written on the 'problems of rural areas', and so perhaps I should simply refer briefly to two underlying trends. The first relates to the transformation of a socio-economic system which was previously based on primary production towards a system based on secondary and increasingly tertiary activities for which urban locations are more important. Coupled with this decline of employment in rural areas has been a rise in expectations, leading to growing dissatisfaction with the range of employment opportunities available. This gap between employment expectations and opportunities in rural areas has found expression in above-average unemployment rates, underemployment and low wages, low female activity rates and high rates of out-migration particularly among young people.

The second trend lies parallel to this: the widening gap between expectations of service provision, and the actual quality of services available. The main forces at work in the contraction of rural service provision relate partly to demand. Not only has there been an absolute decline in population in some areas, but rising *per capita* incomes have increased levels of mobility and have also to some extent accompanied shifts in taste towards higher-level commodities and services which are increasingly satisfied in larger towns. But rural services have also been placed under pressure by changes in the economics of supply. Increasing economies of scale, especially in the retail sector, have tended to raise the levels of support population needed to assure a viable service activity.

These are trends which are clearly discernible, and of course widely known, in many rural areas. But are they *problems* requiring public intervention? Of course many residents of such areas choose to move away to urban centres, and so escape these trends. But a problem remains in the social costs of such decisions. Social and economic opportunities are frequently further reduced for those people who have little real option but to remain behind. This has been seen for example in the impoverishment of rural public transport and possibly also in the ability of rural communities to provide adequate mutual help to their members because of a top-heavy age structure. Some of the externalities arising from such decline accrue directly on the remaining residents in the manner mentioned above, and some impinge on the community at large which has to finance the provision of public services of an acceptable standard despite the increasingly uneconomic nature of the operation.

The need for selectivity

The trends mentioned above present a *prima facie* case for a degree of selectivity between urban centres in the allocation of public investment. Two economic arguments are particularly important in this respect. The first relates to the 'lumpy' nature of public investment: it is simply not possible to provide an equal small amount of, say, further education or hospital provision in each of the 20 or 30 small towns of East Anglia. Second is the importance of agglomeration economies in the operation of many manufacturing companies. The external economies that accompany urban size can play a big part in the selection by industrialists of suitable locations for their plants, and in their subsequent viability. It may be useful in this context to cite the results of a study carried out by the author into the urban size preferences of industrial managers in Thetford and Haverhill, two small expanding towns in East Anglia.[3] The vast majority unequivocally favoured further growth of their towns, largely to increase the pool of labour available to them. This pool would be enlarged both directly by expansion of the population, and indirectly by the attractions that improved urban amenities would have for potential employees. So if one objective of public policy is to improve an area's employment opportunities, there is a case for concentrating public expenditure into a few selected towns.

An approach to selectivity

What criteria might be most appropriate in selecting small towns for positive discrimination? I would suggest that there are four:

(i) growth potential

The potential of a town to achieve successful expansion is an important criterion and might be assessed with reference to a number of factors. First, its location in inter-regional terms: how accessible is it in terms of the needs of potential incoming firms and migrants? Second, its intra-regional location, and its potential ability to serve as an employment and service centre for a wide area. Third, its present endowment of amenities in the widest sense, including not just services but labour pool, etc. Fourth, its recent growth performance which, if carefully interpreted, may to some extent be construed as a surrogate for other more latent elements of growth potential.

(ii) growth capacity

Under this heading it would be necessary to estimate the costs of undertaking growth – costs in a narrow economic sense, and if possible in a broader social and environmental sense too. Probably some variant of urban threshold analysis would be useful in this context. The essential point is to ascertain whether spare capacity exists in the services already installed, or whether excessively costly expenditure would be needed to permit expansion.

(iii) growth need

To examine only a town's potential and capacity for growth would ignore the points made earlier about the pursuit of 'people' rather than 'place' prosperity, and about the need to work from a set of objectives related to previously defined problems. And so some assessment must be made of the ability of a certain amount of investment in each of a number of towns to alleviate such problems as those relating to inadequate employment and service opportunities, discussed above. How many people would benefit? To what extent? And which people? A term coined by Klaasen, 'development worthiness', expresses quite well the combination of measures of potential, capacity and need which I have in mind.

(iv) administrative status

A fourth criterion, which can easily be overlooked by academics or given excessive weight by practitioners, is the administrative framework of the area under consideration. Two points are important. First, some attention ought to be paid at the plan-making stage to the political realities whereby areas discriminated against may successfully sabotage a technically good plan. Second, it is necessary to look at the control of the policy levers whereby policies of discrimination are to be implemented. In the British context both factors appear to me to point to the wisdom of affording at least one selected centre to each of the new county districts that now perform second-tier functions in rural areas. Of particular importance is the power of these district councils in housing matters – an important consideration in the re-fashioning of the distribution of population, as will be discussed later.

If the above four criteria provide guidelines of a general nature in the selection of small towns for positive discrimination, how in the context of a particular rural area is the exercise to be carried out? Clearly it would be necessary to apply alternative weightings to the various factors listed above and thus generate a number of alternative strategies. These would then have to be evaluated against our predetermind list of objectives and in the context of the resources likely to be available. In this way the peculiarities of the local urban system, and of the particular problems it was hoped to alleviate, might be incorporated.

The weakness of the spread effect

Having made a case for selectivity among small towns in the allocation of investment, it would be very satisfactory if powerful spread mechanisms could be relied upon to carry the benefits of such investment out to other small towns and rural areas not directly favoured. But the evidence on this is not at all encouraging. The author has described elsewhere[4] the limited nature of the spatial impact of the two small expanding towns mentioned above, namely Thetford and Haverhill, and it may be useful to summarise these findings.

Three channels of impact were studied, relating to the recruitment of labour, the expenditure of earned income by employees, and the purchase by firms of materials and services. As far as labour recruitment was concerned, the main effects were felt within a 10 to 12 mile radius (or else in cities outside the region). Even firms providing their own transport rarely exceeded this radius. In the expenditure of income, most shopping trips were made either to the expanding towns themselves, or to larger towns such as Norwich and Cambridge. Neighbouring small towns and villages benefited relatively little. And in the purchase of materials and services by firms, 85 or 90 per cent of the impact 'leaked' outside East Anglia. Within the region purchases were made very largely from such big towns as Norwich and Cambridge again, or from other smaller towns in the throes of planned expansion. Once again the majority of small towns and the 'problem' rural areas of East Anglia were very largely unaffected.

Complementary policies in peripheral areas

The implication of all this is that a policy of directing investment to a few selected small towns is likely to generate little economic expansion or personal prosperity beyond its immediate commuting hinterland except in larger centres. Once this is realised, then a question arises concerning the policies that should be pursued in such peripheral areas. It is probably a lack of realisation that equally positive policies are needed for areas discriminated against that has led to the frequent demise of 'growth centre' policies. Fortunately the primacy of a goal of 'people prosperity' rather than 'place prosperity' opens a possible route out of the apparently impossible situation of pursuing a policy of positive spatial discrimination while not neglecting the areas discriminated against.

A number of policies are possible if the goal is to improve the lot of the people presently resident in peripheral areas. First, attempts could be made to build up those aspects of the economy of such areas which do not require an urban location – the primary sector, recreation and tourism, and perhaps retirement migration which brings in a flow of income from other regions.

Second, and perhaps more important, the complementary policy package for peripheral areas should be built around the notion of mobility, in the sense both of migration and of day-to-day mobility. As far as migration is concerned it would seem unjust, having deliberately channelled investment to selected centres, not to give reasonable assistance to those people living outside such centres who might wish to move towards them. Housing is obviously important in this context: the Hunt Report on the Intermediate Areas demonstrated that the inadequate availability of suitable housing is a crucial constraint acting upon people wishing to move in this way.[5] Not only is availability important, but also information about the housing situation, as well as an adequate reception machinery for migrants to the selected centres. This is why I suggested that the extent of the new county districts should be a factor in the process of selecting towns, since housing is a district council matter in this country. Similarly, policies to facilitate job mobility are important – relating to the adequacy of the information on the opportunities available, training and retraining, the reimbursement of expenses incurred in attending interviews, etc.

Regarding mobility in a day-to-day sense, there is a need to look at the requirements of people living beyond the typical ten mile commuting hinterlands of small towns. Encouraging long-distance commuting rather than migration has beneficial economic and social implications for the workers' original places of residence. Perhaps, with their increased involvement in public transport through their preparation of annual Transport Policies and Programmes, county councils may find it worthwhile to encourage commuting over 15 or 20 miles from towns and villages with little prospect of employment growth. Individual firms, acting alone, may find the provision of such transport quite uneconomic.

Finally, mobile services. Possibly much more could be done in this field without excessive subsidy. Already we have mobile libraries, mobile shops, etc. but perhaps there is a need to make information more mobile, in the sense of increasing the awareness of such disadvantaged people as the elderly and the poor of facilities available. This might mean, for example mobile social service offices, spending half a day per week in each of ten villages.

Conclusion

The essential point seems to be that areas of growth and decline must be seen as two sides of the same coin – two necessary aspects of a policy designed to achieve expressed and agreed objectives relating to personal welfare. It may be that the experience of the British town development programme is relevant here. It provides a precedent of 'exporting' authorities such as the GLC working hand-in-hand with 'reception' local authorities in promoting personal welfare objectives by means of integrated housing and employment policies. However such cooperation in a rural context can never be achieved unless the designers of such policies are able to convince elected representatives and others in peripheral areas that such policies are in their interests. This in turn is unlikely to be possible without a full evaluation of the costs and benefits (including the incidence of costs and benefits) of alternative spatial strategies of public investment. And so I see the potential role of small towns in rural areas as one of providing an initial physical framework upon which alternative strategies of development, involving different degrees of discrimination, can be designed and then evaluated.

REFERENCES

1. Lampard, E. E., 'The History of Cities in Economically Advanced Areas', *Economic Development and Cultural Change*, Vol. 3, 1955, pp. 81-136.
2. Hoover, E. M., *An Introduction to Regional Economics*, A. A. Knopf, New York 1971.
3. Moseley, M. J., 'Some Problems of Small Expanding Towns', *Town Planning Review*, Vol. 44, 1973, pp. 263-78.
4. Moseley, M. J., 'The Impact of Growth Centres in Rural Regions. II An Analysis of Spatial Flows in East Anglia'. *Regional Studies*, Vol. 7, No. 1, 1973, pp. 77-94.
5. Hunt, Sir Joseph, *Report of a Committee on the Intermediate Areas*, Cmnd. 3998, H.M.S.O., London 1969.

5. Rural Settlement Policy: Problems and Conflicts

JOHN B. AYTON

Problems and Needs

This chapter examines the problems relating to planning policies for rural settlement in the context of changes taking place, and the social and economic implications of these policies, with particular reference to Norfolk county in eastern England.[1]

In Norfolk, economic growth has tended to concentrate around the major urban centres and the town development areas, leaving a large rural area outside the immediate influence of these centres. This rural area includes some 14 small towns and 400 villages and accounts for about 40 per cent of the total county population – the small towns accounting for a quarter of the rural population. It is not, however, a static situation. In the 1950s rural decline was widespread, but through the 1960s population growth has gradually spread outwards from the major centres to include a large part of the county.[2]

These population increases in the 1960s were not, however, supported by a corresponding expansion of local employment and indeed, throughout this period, substantial decline in male employment was recorded. This was due chiefly to the loss of about 8,000 male jobs in the primary sector which was only partially counteracted by the provision of alternative employment. Overall, there were 3,000 fewer jobs for men in 1971 than in 1961.

Despite the general run-down in employment opportunities, unemployment has not been particularly high, and even where the rate has been high (it has reached 8 per cent) the absolute number of people involved has been small. Thus, the Hunt Committee

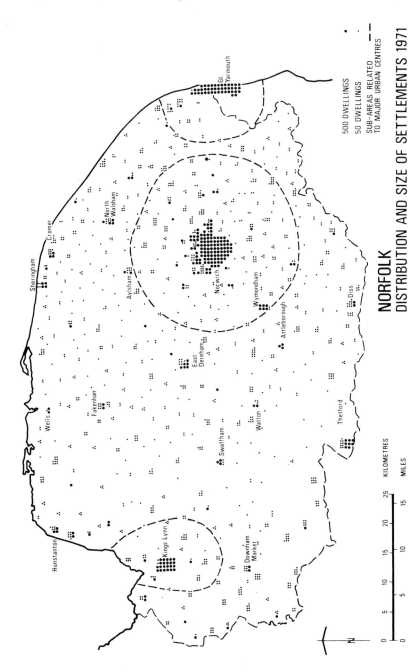

NORFOLK
DISTRIBUTION AND SIZE OF SETTLEMENTS 1971

500 DWELLINGS
50 DWELLINGS
SUB-AREAS RELATED
TO MAJOR URBAN CENTRES

Gt. Yarmouth

North Walsham

Sheringham

Cromer

Aylsham

Norwich

Wymondham

Diss

Attleborough

East Dereham

Wells

Fakenham

Swaffham

Watton

Thetford

Hunstanton

Kings Lynn

Downham Market

KILOMETRES

MILES

N

were not impressed that the scale of the problem warranted special action by central government. Nevertheless, certain sections of the population have employment difficulties. For example, a recent analysis carried out for the remote Fakenham and Diss areas showed that a high proportion of the unemployed were older and unskilled men.[3] Similarly, less than 30 per cent of grammar school leavers manage to obtain local jobs, with girls experiencing particular difficulty. Although secondary-modern leavers appear to fare better, it is not easy to determine whether the quality of choice is adequate and there is some evidence that school leavers accept local jobs below the level of their abilities.[4] Local opinion and local groups constantly refer to the loss of the young and most able people in the community, and certainly this has been the experience in the past (the numbers in the 20–29 age group in 1971 are 30 per cent below the 0–9 age group in 1951). The run-down in job opportunities had thus led to a gradual increase in longer distance commuting to the major centres and also to population movements away from the more remote areas.

An analysis of Census data points to areas with particular problems. For example, areas around Swaffham, Fakenham, North Walsham and Diss have a high proportion of unskilled and semi-skilled workers. Similarly, the proportion of poor housing is higher than average, car ownership is low and the proportions of elderly people and children are high. The latter sections of the population are of course especially vulnerable to any decrease in the level of public and private services, and particularly public transport.

Much of the rest of the rural area falls into a second category of 'need' in that the population is also relatively poor and badly housed, but tends to have a higher car ownership and a smaller proportion of elderly people than the worst areas. An analysis of the 1971 Census shows that the prosperous areas, with a higher than average proportion of skilled, professional and managerial workers, owner–occupiers and car owners, have spread outwards from the urban centres. There have also been improvements in the early 1970s in the general situation where small towns have attracted industrial development and new population. Therefore, the general difference between the 'poverty' of the rural areas and the 'prosperity' related to the major urban centres and the town development areas, although still present, has become less distinct.

Resource constraints

The opportunities for change in the rural situation are constrained and influenced by the existing physical infrastructure, in terms of the settlement pattern, systems of public utilities and communications networks, and the resources available for modifying it. While it is difficult to anticipate the level of financial resources that will be available, it is clear that they will, for some time, be limited, and planning policies must be framed within the context of what is feasible, or reasonably likely. Those services which are financed from the rates (e.g. education, highways, sewerage, water) will be much more of a constraint than those which are 'self supporting' and budgeted nationally (e.g. electricity, gas, telephones). Investment choices and priorities must be made in those sectors which can influence policy-making in a more restrictive and specific way than the general aim of minimising public expenditure. For example, the new education authority will need to choose between investing in the re-modelling or replacement of old schools (there are nearly 300 pre-1903 schools and about 500 mobile classrooms); in reorganisation, providing middle schools (over 100 would be needed); in extending technical education, and in catering for growth in school population at all levels. The present allocation by the Department of Education and Science is related only to a 'roofs over heads' policy, and is barely adequate for that. Embargoes on new residential development are currently operating in several towns and villages and more may be necessary because of inadequate school accommodation.

In rural Norfolk there are a large number of small villages without sewerage. Several towns are in urgent need of extensions, and there is a need for new works to cater for growth, particularly around Norwich and Great Yarmouth. Similar considerations apply in relation to water supplies, but perhaps less critically. The Transportation Budget must choose between investment in by-passes round towns and villages, improvements to inter-urban roads, improvements to rural and urban roads and public transport subsidies. Social services, with a fairly low investment in fixed infrastructure, are less critical in this context, but the running costs of the service can become an important factor. With regard to the statutory undertakers' services, the 'choice' element is less evident, although gas services will not be extended unless it can be done economically (i.e. to serve large-scale development) and where the cost of extending the telephone service is high, the waiting list may be long.

With resources limited (and shrinking) policies must attempt to make the most effective use of what there is, and development, particularly residential, must be related to education, health, transportation and public utility programmes, both in time and location.

Policy options

Development and investment policies have 'social' implications in their impact on individuals and communities, and planning policies have 'social benefit' objectives. Some objectives, such as those relating to accessibility to opportunities and facilities are fairly easily measured, and the effect of alternative policies can be assessed. But other 'social' objectives, particularly those which refer to 'community life' or 'social balance', are much less tangible and less easily defined, so that the effects of possible policies are more difficult to assess. Rural planning is particularly susceptible to these, based usually on concepts (valid or otherwise) of what life in villages and small towns is, or has been. Not only are these difficult to assess in quantitative terms, but the extent to which planning policies affect them at all is debatable. These economic and social aspects of planning policies are discussed firstly in relation to the small towns, and, secondly, to the policies for villages.

The small towns

The populations of the 14 small towns range up to 10,000 but are generally between 3,000 and 5,000 and they are interspersed at fairly regular intervals among a widespread pattern of villages. The basis for this pattern was the original Anglo-Saxon settlement, related to agriculture, which adjusted to the needs of the mid-nineteenth century, but not the twentieth. From this scatter, a pattern of market centres emerged, but there are now only two major agricultural markets, Norwich and King's Lynn, with one or two small town markets surviving on a modest scale and in a semi-specialist role.

Since the inter-war period the fortunes of the small towns have depended much more on the extent to which they managed to attract industrial development. Decline before the war was associated with agricultural depression and the agricultural revival after the war tended to pass by the small towns because it was associated with the labour run-down, population decline and an increasing tendency to look to the larger centres for services. The small towns have been identified as occupying the key role of any policy for the rural areas by many people over a long time. They are centres for shopping, secondary education, professional services and, increasingly, for employment in jobs in industry and services to replace those lost in agriculture. This was recognised in the studies by the East Anglian Consultative Committee and the Economic Planning Council. The *Small Towns Study* further confirmed the role and the significance of these towns. It showed that the more remote towns were in danger of losing ground, with services on the margin of viability because of declining catchment populations. This is perhaps less true now, but the view that the towns could become 'growth points' to bolster the economy of the rural areas and widen opportunities remains valid.

The *Small Towns Study* showed the sort of investment thresholds that applied in Diss, Dereham and Fakenham and which influence the possibilities of their being treated as rural growth points. Similar critical factors have been identified in each of the other towns in the county, and in virtually every case utility services have little spare capacity and new investment would be needed to back up the selection of any of these towns as a growth point. Some have already reached a critical level, where major new investment is urgently needed just to keep things moving. If one or two towns are selected in the Structure Plan as growth points, they will have to compete for new investment between each other, with major centres and with the rest of the rural area; certainly resources will not be available for all the small towns together. It has also become clear that the towns with the 'easy' physical potential are not those in the areas of greatest social need, but there is a choice in that investment can be steered to any town that is selected.

Environmental objectives on the other hand can impose a total constraint, where the architectural or historic character would be seriously affected by growth, for example where the town centres have very limited capacity to accommodate traffic and car parking without serious detriment to their aesthetic quality, as at Aylsham, Diss, Wymondham and Fakenham.

The villages

There are about 400 villages in the rural area, the rest being within the 'pressure' areas around the major centres. All but one or two are mentioned in Domesday (together with a further 150 which have now virtually disappeared). They all, therefore, have a long history, grew rapidly in the early nineteenth century, and then declined with the agricultural depression right up to the post-war period, and most of them up to the 1960s. Between 1951 and 1961, for example, over 300 villages showed a population decline.

Until the post-war period, the majority of villages were substantially self-sufficient in terms of employment, shopping, schooling, health and other facilities that were available. Gradually, since the war, rising standards and economic forces have tended to shift the services away, either to a central village or more likely to the local market town or major centres. The post-1944 Education Act reorganisation took secondary school children out of the village school and 80 village primary schools have been closed. Studies of village shops indicate that their number fell by 50 per cent between 1950 and the mid-60s, and the resident village policeman and district nurse have virtually disappeared.[5] Few villages now have rail services, and, although bus services are still fairly widespread, the level of services has declined significantly.

About 66 per cent of the villages are below 500 in population and 44 per cent below 300. Only 11 per cent are over 1,000 and only a few reach the 3,000 population level. It is the small size of the average village that is critical in terms of the services and facilities that can be expected in each one. Studies carried out by the Planning Department of Norfolk County Council have identified critical thresholds related to various services. For example, at the 300-500 population level, it is estimated that the village can support a shop, a pub and a school with between 30 and 50 pupils. But a primary school with 100 pupils, a fairly economic level, requires a support population of 1,000, while a 'middle' school of 240 pupils requires a population of 4,000. Each doctor has to have at least 2,000 patients and so a practice of three doctors needs a support population of about 6,000. A regular surgery seems to be viable only where the village population exceeds 1,800. A district nurse is provided for 3,000 population and chemists are provided on the basis of a 4,000 to 4,500 population catchment. Earlier studies have shown that butchers and bakers need populations of between 1,500 and 3,000.

As with towns, aesthetic considerations and the character of the rural environment will influence village development policies. There are widespread differences of character within the rural area and, in some parts of it, it would generally be accepted that the architectural and historical character of the villages is such that modern development on any significant scale would not be appropriate, and that the villages should be preserved in their present form. Over much more of the rural area, the intrinsic architectural merit is not so strong that it should be a constraint on future development, but for many people the small village in its rural setting has a quality that should be protected and preserved in that form.

The services infrastructure (sewerage, water, gas, electricity, telephone) is critical because a development policy which would require major new investment spread over a large number of villages would not be feasible. Our studies have sought to define the capacity that already exists or can reasonably be anticipated and also, by sample studies, to quantify the investment implications of alternative development policies, comparing the effects of dispersal and concentration.

Water and electricity were spread through the rural area during the 1950s, and sewerage schemes had become fairly widespread through the 1960s. Nevertheless, nearly 300 villages are still without a sewerage scheme and the spare capacity in the existing systems is very limited. The road system over much of the rural area still consists of country lanes, without footpaths, and, if development is spread wide, the traffic pressures on these roads would lead to demands for widenings and straightenings. Although there are many village schools with spare accommodation, continued dispersal would increase school transport costs, particularly if related to a system of middle schools, and annual school transport expenditure in the County is already approaching a million pounds. Many services such as telephones, electricity, postal services, water, schools and school transport, are provided at a standard cost or at no direct cost to the consumer. However, the actual costs are well above average and all are subsidised directly or indirectly. In some instances, where services are provided at a high cost, the standard of provision is significantly lower than in urban or suburban areas and mobile services generally (such as libraries) cannot provide the same degree of services as fixed-point services, although the *per capita* costs are higher.

Thus, the economic factors point to the advantages of concentration and selection, and because the provision of social facilities cannot ignore economic realities these are, in a sense, 'social' arguments too for such policies. Although concentration and selection would need to be backed by programmes to maintain reasonable social services in settlements not selected (e.g. mobile libraries, health visitors, meals-on-wheels and public transport) it would not seem sensible to accept development where it would add to the numbers of people in the smaller villages who would have to depend upon such services, imposing extra cost to receive a lower level of service.

To be effective, a non-dispersal policy should prevent incremental and piecemeal dispersed development, and should be applied strictly because, with only a few houses in each village per year, over 15–20 years there is capacity for 30,000 houses spread over the whole area. This is much greater than any current projection of housing or population, and therefore, potentially, totally prejudicial to effective rationalisation. But, if such policies are accepted, this would leave most villages without significant new development or direct investment, raising the spectre of the 'dying' village and the decline of village life, and a considerable limitation on freedom of choice. Of course, changes in social life are taking place quite independently of planning policies, and the social life of a community is not entirely a function of size. The decline of traditional village institutions, where it occurs, can be as much due to changing interests as changing population. New housing development may not bring new 'life' to a village, and may on the contrary create conflicts. The arguments themselves are conflicting and the evidence thin. Thus, in order to understand better the consequences of planning policies in this context, there is a great need for a continuing programme of research as part of the monitoring process.

With regard to the freedom of choice which concentration policies allow, the choice denied to most would be that of living in a new house in a small village. The choice is not wide open in that the individual must opt for a small village or direct access to services – he cannot get both together. Some are, of course, willing to accept the low level of services, but it is not true of everybody, and policies must indicate clearly what is expected for each village not only for investment programmes, but to allow the individual to make an informed choice.

Conclusions

It appears that rural Norfolk is approaching stability in relation to employment. Agriculture now forms a small part of the employment base and adjustments in this sector are becoming much less significant as a factor leading to decline. Although the rate of decline is not large-scale or dramatic, problem areas remain, and a case for stimulating the economy of the rural areas can be justified.

Services for the scattered population are costly to provide and maintain and, with limited resources, it appears that effective provision can only be made on the basis of selective and coordinated investment, both public and private. The Structure Plan provides the only statutory planning framework for this purpose. The small towns are the only centres likely to attract new employment and be capable of sustaining anything other than very basic services. With limited resources, selection is thus imperative. With the large number and wide scatter of small villages the need for selectivity in relation to village development policies is even greater.

REFERENCES

1. Since this paper was prepared, a number of forecasts have been revised in the light of changing demographic assumptions and economic conditions, and a Draft Structure Plan has been published in April, 1976. For further details of matters discussed in this paper see *The Rural Area: Strategic Choices*, a Structure Plan Discussion Paper, Norfolk County Council, June 1975.

2. An extrapolation of recent trends suggests that the rural area could attract about 25 per cent of the total county population growth (20,000 people) by 1990. This will comprise a mixture of natural increase, job-led migration, those commuting to urban areas and retirement. See *Norfolk County Planning Department Surveys*, Norwich.

3. East Anglia Consultative Committee, *Small Towns Study*, Ipswich 1972.

4. *Norfolk County Planning Department Surveys*, Norwich.

5. *Ibid.*

6. Agencies for Rural Development in Scotland*

D. C. NICHOLLS

There is, of course, a large variety of agencies concerned with aspects of rural development in Scotland. The Scottish Office, under the Secretary of State for Scotland, embraces departments such as the Scottish Development Department and the Department of Agriculture and Fisheries for Scotland, and many other United Kingdom government departments have relevant responsibilities, for instance, the Department of Industry. There are statutory local authorities and voluntary local associations, such as the North East Scotland Development Authority and the Isle of Arran Development Association. The Development Commission, the Small Industries Council for Rural Areas of Scotland and many other bodies are concerned in various ways with promoting and fostering small industries, craft industries, and so on.[1]

It is not my purpose here to attempt a comprehensive survey of these agencies. Rather I propose to look at two types of agency which are of particular importance, not only in the Scottish context, but also because of a possible wider applicability to other parts of the United Kingdom. Firstly, I shall give a brief survey of the work of the Highlands and Islands Development Board, an *ad hoc* body, appointed not elected, the first regional authority in Britain to be given real powers of economic development. Secondly, I want to look forward to May 1975 and beyond, to the new regional authorities which will emerge following local government reorganisation in Scotland. For many of these authorities any planning and development activity will be predominantly rural in its context: what kind of activity might be expected or desired from these authorities?

The Highland Region

It is necessary to give some background information about the

69

Highlands to provide a general context for understanding the work of the Development Board. It is important to appreciate the very great contrast between the Highlands and Islands of Scotland and the rural areas of Southern Britain. There are those in East Anglia who think of north Norfolk as a large remote area, but compared to the region covered by the Highlands and Islands Development Board, the description really takes on a very different meaning.

The Highland Board area covers what are known as the seven crofting counties — Shetland, Orkney, Caithness, Sutherland, Ross and Cromarty, Inverness and Argyll. The extent of the area from the Mull of Kintyre in the south west to Muckle Flugga in the north of the Shetland Islands is something over 400 miles, or rather more than the distance from Edinburgh to London. Few people realise that setting off from Glasgow Airport to fly to the Highlands you may, if you wish, proceed in a south-westerly direction and you will eventually reach the airstrip at Campbeltown in the south of Argyll. The region covers about nine million acres (3.6 million hectares), which is almost one-half of the area of Scotland and approximately one-sixth of the area of Great Britain. A glance at a physical map reveals the basic upland nature of the mainland part of the region, with for the most part only a very narrow coastal strip below 500 feet (152 metres). A significant part of the region is comprised of islands. This topography has obvious consequences for settlement patterns, for communications, for agriculture, and so on. The region exhibits a very wide diversity of climatic conditions: in the Cairngorms in the east there is now a flourishing winter sports season, while subtropical gardens flourish at various points on the west coast. The rainfall near the southern edge of the Highlands around the north of Loch Lomond, for example, is something over 125 inches (320 cm.) per annum while at Inverness and around the Moray Firth the climate is among the driest and sunniest to be found in Great Britain.

It should be remembered, particularly by anyone concerned with attempts at social and economic development in the region, that the topographical and climatic diversity is parallelled by a diversity of peoples. A man from Easter Ross is very different from a native of the Mull of Kintyre; the Shetlander is readily distinguished from the Lewis man. Different parts of the region, in short, have different cultures, different traditions, different personal characteristics, and all these differences need to be borne in mind in any consideration of the future welfare and

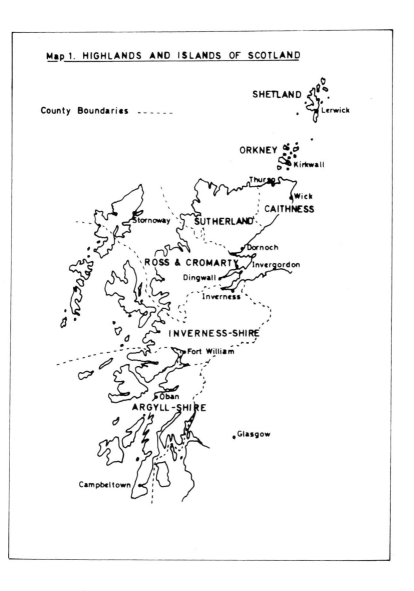

Map 1. HIGHLANDS AND ISLANDS OF SCOTLAND

County Boundaries - - - - - -

SHETLAND

Lerwick

ORKNEY

Kirkwall

Thurso

Wick

CAITHNESS

Stornoway SUTHERLAND

Dornoch

ROSS & CROMARTY Invergordon

Dingwall

Inverness

INVERNESS-SHIRE

Fort William

Oban

ARGYLL-SHIRE

Glasgow

Campbeltown

development of the area.

The population of the Highlands and Islands in 1971 was recorded at approximately 280,000, which represented a small increase of some 5,000 on the 1961 Census figure. This was the first intercensal increase since 1841, at which time the population of the region was nearly 400,000. The present figure represents about 5 per cent of the population of Scotland and about 0.5 per cent of the population of Great Britain. The average density of population throughout the Highlands is a mere 20 persons per square mile. It is perhaps salutary to recall that at the peak levels of overcrowding in the City of Glasgow there would have been nearly as many people in one square mile as there are today in the whole of the Highlands! Approximately one-third of the Highland population live around the Moray Firth (including 30,000 in Inverness) and a further third reside on the islands. About two-fifths live in settlements of more than 1,000 people and another one-fifth form the crofting population, mainly in the north and west of the region.

For most people, the basic problem of the Highlands and Islands can be summed up in a single word – *depopulation*. Depopulation has been a feature of the region for a century and a half at least, and the plain fact is that, even today, the primary industries on which the peoples of the Highlands are heavily dependent cannot support a self-sustaining social and economic life in the many small, ageing and isolated communities; decline therefore continues in many areas. In spite of an increase of more than one third in the employment in manufacturing industries in the Highlands over the last ten years, the manufacturing sector still accounts for only something like 12 to 15 per cent of employment compared to 43 per cent in the whole of Scotland; 10 to 12 per cent of the labour force of the Highlands are engaged in primary industries and over 70 per cent are in service industries. The unemployment pattern has shown relatively little change over the last ten years, fluctuating on a seasonal basis from 6 to 10 per cent – falling to 6 per cent for the peak months of the summer tourist season and rising regularly each winter to at least the 10 per cent level. There has been some slight improvement relative to other parts of the United Kingdom in the last two or three years but little absolute improvement was felt in the region until very recently when some of the exciting developments associated with the exploitation of North Sea oil began to have some effect. For a number of years average earnings in the Highlands have been of the order of 13 per cent below the British average.

These various facts and figures about the region indicate something of the scale of the problem which the Highlands and Islands Development Board was set up to tackle, but before turning to a consideration of the work of the Board over the last eight years there is a further historical strand of the background which should be mentioned. In a short time one cannot give an adequate account of the relevant social and economic history of the region, but the starting point really has to be the famous Battle of Culloden in 1746, the last battle to be fought on British soil, when the Duke of Cumberland's troops finally crushed the Jacobite Rebellion led by Bonnie Prince Charlie. (In view of recent political events in Scotland perhaps one might now say that the view of that battle as the final crushing of the Jacobites was a mistaken one!) Nevertheless in the second half of the eighteenth century there was a significant opening up and development of many parts of the Highlands in the face of a growing demand in the south of Britain for many of the products of the region – wool, cattle, oats, fish and the products of the kelp industry which came to be particularly important for soap and glass making. However, the closing years of the eighteenth century and the first quarter of the nineteenth century saw the collapse of most of the Highland economy apart, notably, from the wool trade. As a consequence, the Highlands experienced extensive migration. On the one hand, there was what might euphemistically be called 'voluntary' migration, particularly from the western parts of the region and most of all, perhaps, from the Outer Hebrides – areas where there were simply far more people than the local economy could support; and, secondly, there was 'compulsory' migration as a result of the now infamous 'clearances'. In essence, sheep were given priority over the interests of agricultural tenants and far fewer men were needed to look after the sheep than formerly farmed the land.[2]

For the past century and more, then, there has been a succession of government measures designed to protect and subsidise many aspects of the Highland way of life and many sections of the Highland community. For example, crofting tenants, nearly a hundred years ago, were given what virtually amounts to perpetual security of tenure of the land – the land on which their house stands together, typically, with a few acres of arable land and common grazing rights. Most crofting tenants have long since ceased to work their crofts on a full-time basis and indeed many crofts have never provided anything other than part-time employment as an ancillary to fishing or some other local industry.[3] Special assistance has been available for the construction and improvement of crofter housing; low interest loans have been obtainable since 1912 and since 1948 extra grants for the improvement of houses have been available over and above the house improvement grants which are generally applicable throughout Britain. There is a very high standard of provision of basic infrastructure and services throughout the Highlands compared with most remote regions in Western Europe.[4] Electricity, for example, is connected to 98 per cent of premises in the region. The North of Scotland Hydro-Electric Board, formed in 1943, has achieved a great deal in 30 years and of course it had social and economic objectives as well as the generation of power for the national grid. Ninety-eight per cent of the population are linked to a public water supply and 90 per cent are connected to a public sewage disposal system. Whilst a tourist in August may question the view that the roads and ferries in the region are adequate, there can be little doubt that they are nevertheless of a relatively high standard.

In all these measures there has been little specific attention given to *economic development*; rather these policies have been pursued for social and political reasons – or, as some would say, to expiate the guilt of the Southerner. Perhaps the aims of government policy are still primarily political and social (or at least were so until the discovery of oil under the North Sea) but there is no doubt at all that a much more specific development focus was provided by the passing of the Highlands and Islands Development Act in 1965.

The Highlands and Islands Development Board[5]

The seven members of the Board (four full-time, three part-time) are appointed by the Secretary of State for Scotland. The Board now has a staff of over 200 – some light-hearted remarks have been made about the Board setting a good example by being one of the biggest growth sectors of employment in Inverness!

The Board has two broad objectives: (1) to assist the people of the Highlands and Islands to improve their economic and social conditions; (2) to enable the Highlands and Islands to play a more effective part in the economic and social development of Great

Britain. These objectives are unexceptionable and all-embracing. The difficulties start when one begins to translate them into practice and to formulate and carry through a programme of action which will secure at least partial fulfilment of these objectives, or, as the first Chairman of the Board, Sir Robert Grieve, put it, when one 'exchanges the unexceptionable sentiment for the terror of action'.

The Board has wide-ranging powers, including powers to acquire land, to build factories and to provide services and equipment for these factories; to advance loans or make grants for 'any activity which will contribute to the economic or social development of the Highlands and Islands'; to take a share in the equity of companies which the Board assists financially; to provide a range of advisory and other services for firms, individuals and organisations in the region – management services, marketing assistance, publicity advice and so on; and to carry out and commission surveys and research.

General policy

The general strategy of the Board from its inception has been to assist anything with job-making potential, no matter how small. (It is important to keep in mind the scale of most of the communities in the region – a mere handful of new jobs, which would be insignificant in relation to Scottish or even Highland employment figures, may nevertheless make a very significant impact on a high level of unemployment in a small community). The Board set out from the beginning to engage in what has been termed 'a multitude of fruitful actions' and has given various forms of assistance to industries and activities of all sizes all over the region. The Board has aimed to back local initiative, to restore among the peoples of the region faith in the future of the region and faith in the future of their own communities, and to overcome a certain understandable mistrust of, and even hostility towards, the Board itself.

Early in its existence, the Board adopted a series of general policies relating to the main sectors of employment in the region:

Agriculture. It was recognised that there was scope for increased production from agriculture in the Highlands, but it was equally clear that employment in agriculture would continue to decline and must necessarily do so if the agricultural work force were to

75

achieve what might be regarded as a reasonable standard of living. Indeed, in the space of five years from 1966 the full-time agricultural labour force in the region fell by over one third to around 4,000. The contribution of crofting to the gross output of Highland agriculture is something like 20 per cent, although of course in some parts of the region its significance is very much greater. Essentially, however, crofting is very much more important as a way of life, for it is largely a part-time and inherently unstable form of agriculture. Nevertheless it is recognised as having an important role to play in maintaining a 'living countryside' and indeed it is probably the best system for keeping something like the present numbers of people in what is very difficult territory. The aim of the Board in relation to crofting has been particularly to assist in the provision of a wider range of alternative employment to which crofters can turn as their main source of income.

Fishing. Traditionally fishing has been very important in many parts of the region. Much money and effort has been devoted towards reviving the fishing industry among island and other communities, and the Board has assisted with the provision of boats, the training of crews, and the setting up of essential fish processing plant. Over eight years, more than £3 million have been spent by the Board, and late in 1973 the Chairman announced a new five-year programme of aid to the fishing industry which would amount to approximately £4 million.[6] Considerable success has already been achieved in the redevelopment of some of the traditional fishing ports, and many fishing communities which had long since experienced decline are now once more alive and flourishing.[7]

Forestry. It was thought that forestry was likely to have increasing importance in providing employment opportunities in the Highlands, both in the silvicultural stages of the industry and, perhaps more significantly, in the wood processing industries. The Forestry Commission already have nearly half a million acres (200,000 hectares) of plantations in the Highlands and in recent years have demonstrated that trees may be established successfully on soils which were once thought to be most unsuitable for forests.[8] The Board have cooperated with the Commission in many areas regarding matters such as the search for appropriate sites for further afforestation.

Tourism. One of the greatest, if not the greatest, natural resources of the Highlands and Islands is the unique scenic qualities of the region – a region which is in fact one of the last open areas in Western Europe. The Highland Board saw possibilities of making a quick impact in the tourist sector of the economy and engaged in many activities right from the beginning. The Board has carried through a series of massive publicity campaigns. It was recognised that there was a need for further accommodation in the region and in this connection, most notably, the Board are in process of developing five hotels at different points in the west of the region, the first two of which are now open on the Isle of Mull and the Isle of Barra. Projects which may qualify for financial assistance from the Board include new hotels, hotel or guest house extensions and improvements, provision of self-catering accommodation, and touring caravan and camping sites. Other needs include the extension of the season beyond the traditional two or three months of the summer and the dissemination of information about the region and the facilities which it offers to the tourist, both in terms of general publicity and in relation to visitors already in the area. The Board has assisted, for instance, the promotion of specific activity holidays (for example golf or fishing) and special events outside the main tourist seasons (such as the Spey Valley Ski Festival in February and the Wester Ross Festival of the Countryside in May) and has been very active in setting up and encouraging a large number of local tourist associations and tourist information centres throughout the region. Other services provided by the Board have included coordinating public transport facilities and the publication of a composite timetable of public transport in the region, and the negotiation of cut prices with hoteliers and others to encourage visitors in the spring and the autumn. Something like two million people visit the Highlands each year spending now between £40 and £50 million in the region. These figures are increasing by something like 5 per cent per annum it is thought, and the tourist related industries now occupy more than 10 per cent of the region's work force.[9]

Manufacturing industry. This sector of employment was rightly regarded as most important of all and the extent to which the manufacturing sector could be expanded would be crucial to the success of the whole series of policies for the development of the region. Nearly £5 million of grants and loans has been spent in this field by the Highland Board and it has engaged in vigorous promotion activity to persuade industrialists to consider sites in the Highlands as possible locations for new developments.

The strategy of the Board has centred around three important industrial growth areas stretching from the Fort William/Lochaber area at the southern end of the Great Glen (including the location of the £15 million Wiggins Teape pulp and paper mill which opened in 1965 just before the Highland Board was set up), through the largest growth area around the Moray Firth, including Inverness, to the Caithness growth area which was given particular stimulus by the developments of the United Kingdom Atomic Energy Authority at Dounreay in the late 1950s and 1960s. But it was around the Moray Firth that the greatest potential for development lay – potential deriving particularly from the deep water port facilities which would be possible, the expanses of flat land adjacent to the water, and the availability of abundant supplies of water and electricity. The Highland Board, in association with local authorities, commissioned a report from planning consultants on the feasibility of expanding the population of the Moray Firth area to around 200,000.[10] From the beginning, the Board was anxious to secure one or two major industrial developments in the area which might trigger off further developments in due course. The Board fought hard and successfully to secure for Invergordon on the Moray Firth the British Aluminium Company smelter which commenced working in 1971. The £37 million smelter received no finance from the Highland Board, but received financial assistance directly from the Department of Trade and Industry and is a key element in the Board's strategy for the development of the Moray Firth. Other proposals for the area included a possible chemical works but some of the original ideas have been rapidly overtaken by events associated with the discovery of oil under the North Sea.

At the same time as seeking to concentrate major industrial growth in the three main areas just described, the Board was concerned to establish a series of minor growth areas or holding points in the west and on the Islands. The Board recognised the danger and indeed the continuing reality of migration within the region from west to east. The members recognised that the Board would be judged ultimately according to its success or otherwise in stemming migration from the west and from the Islands, and not simply according to any success it might have in stimulating major developments in the east of the region. Measures taken have ranged from assistance to traditional industries, such as the Shetland knitwear industry and the tweed industry in the Outer Hebrides, to new small scale industries, often labour-intensive and producing a high value/low weight product, thus minimising transport costs for both raw materials and finished products.

Financial assistance

In the first eight years of its existence the Highlands and Islands Development Board expended over £16 million in grants and loans in assisting the development of the region (Table 1). About 44 per cent of this total was in the form of grants.

Table 1: H.I.D.B. Assistance to October 31, 1973.

| | (£ thousands) | | | |
	Grants	Loans	Total	% all assistance
Tourism	3,569	1,509	5,078	31
Manufacturing	1,929	3,008	4,937	30
Fisheries	607	2,570	3,177	20
Agriculture	117	1,323	1,440	8
Non-economic	340	—	340	2
Other	683	921	1,604	9
Total	7,245	9,331	16,576	100
% all assistance	44	56	100	

Source: Tourism in the Highlands and Islands, H.I.D.B., February 1974.

The 2 per cent categorised as non-economic grants represents small payments made from time to time for social reasons with no prospect of direct economic returns. One such grant went to assist a part-time hairdresser on the grounds that if the morale of the women of the locality were not maintained then further pressure would be put upon the men to leave and seek employment elsewhere.

The Board estimates that the assistance provided has attracted more than an equivalent amount of private capital – something of the order of £20 million over the same eight-year period. It is estimated that over 8,000 new jobs have been created directly as a result of assistance from the Board, which works out at something like £2,000 per job, though it must be remembered that more than half of this cost, on average, had been in the form of a loan and will hopefully be recovered in due course.

It has sometimes been suggested that the Board has exceeded the normal functions of a public body in providing risk capital whereas the usual practice is for public capital to follow when private capital has given a lead. But the fundamental reason for the existence of the Board is that private capital has failed to give an adequate lead in the region, and it is only with the prospect of highly profitable exploitation of North Sea oil that private capital has begun to flow into the region without special prompting and assistance.

The Board has consistently sought to minimise risk by paying particular attention to *local* initiative, and its Management Services branch provides 'after-care' to projects in receipt of financial assistance. In the first seven years of the Board, 66 of the 820 ventures assisted with loans failed or ceased trading, which represented about 10 per cent of the total loans advanced by the Board. In such an operation, this may be regarded not as a high proportion but as a surprisingly low percentage loss.

It must be borne in mind that the financial assistance available directly from the Highland Board is fairly limited in scale: large scale assistance for major developments has always come direct from central government. The maximum amount which the Board is permitted to advance solely on its own initiative in a combination of grant and loan is £75,000, which may be increased to £150,000 with the official approval of the Secretary of State for Scotland. Over and above that figure the consent of the Treasury is required, which is tantamount to removing the grant-giving powers from the Board where large sums of money are involved.

North Sea oil

With the feverish activity connected with the exploration for, and proposed exploitation of, oil and gas reserves under the North Sea, which is now, in 1974, a common feature of life in Scotland, it is difficult to realise that oil-related developments did not affect the Highlands in any direct way until 1972. The Scottish base for earlier exploration was Aberdeen. However, by the middle of 1974, two oil production platform fabrication yards were in operation on the shores of the Moray Firth and a further three yards were proposed for that area. Three or four others were in various stages of planning or development in different parts of the Highlands from Ardyne Point on the Firth of Clyde to Dunnet Bay near John O'Groats. The first half of 1974 saw a protracted public inquiry into a proposal for a fabrication yard on Loch Carron on the west coast. Other oil-related activities include supply bases in the Shetlands, the coating of pipes for submarine pipelines at Invergordon, and proposals for oil terminals in both the Orkney and Shetland Islands. In the latter case, the local planning authority sought extensive powers to acquire land which might be needed for development in order to secure a greater measure of control than might be possible using normal planning control procedures.

There is, then, the prospect of literally thousands of new jobs in the Highlands and Islands as a result of the development of the United Kingdom petroleum industry. Developments on this scale and at such speed bring severe problems of servicing and infrastructure provision which have put some of the local authorities involved under considerable strain. More fundamentally, there are problems concerned with achieving a balance between conservation and development, and some also talk of 'social pollution' – problems arising when large concentrations of people are imported into a region to cope with work which is quite beyond the scope of the indigenous labour force. Some of the problems which are considerable in the east of the region will be exacerbated if and when developments take place along the west coast. It remains to be seen how far developments are permitted on the west, but it is clear that if discoveries of oil are made to the west of the Orkneys and perhaps even to the west of the Hebrides, then pressures for development on the west coast will be enormous.[11]

The future of the Board

The latest forecasts indicate that the United Kingdom might well become an oil exporting country by the early 1980s, with production in excess of 150 million tons a year.[12] It is now reasonable to assume, and no longer a fanciful dream, that the Highlands and Islands will become a 'boom' region within the next few years – though the distribution of prosperity across the region is another matter. By 1980 one may well be looking somewhere south of the Highland Boundary Fault to find what is then the problem region of the United Kingdom. When that stage is reached it may well be felt that the task of the Highlands and Islands Development Board is complete and the *raison d'être* of the Board has disappeared.

It will be suggested in the next part of this paper, however, that there is a case for an earlier transfer of the powers and duties of the Board to local authorities. Although the task of the Board is uncompleted and the need for the kind of work it has performed remains, the time is ripe to consider strengthening the new Scottish regional authorities, rather than retaining an appointed development agency alongside, but independent of, an elected regional council. This suggestion derives not from any view of the Highland Board as a failure: quite the reverse. It is the very success of the Board in demonstrating convincingly that its functions can be exercised at a regional level which gives the argument credibility. It was essential that such an innovation in regional planning should be made on an *ad hoc* basis, but the performance of the Board has pointed the way for other areas. All the regions of Scotland have, in varying degrees, problems of social and economic development. One should not envisage a network of nine or twelve development boards in parallel with the regional authorities – to which attention must now be turned.

New regional authorities

The pattern of local government in Scotland which will emerge in May 1975 is essentially a two-tier structure, with nine regions as the top tier, and 53 district authorities forming the lower tier. In addition, there will be three all-purpose authorities for the principal island areas – Shetland, Orkney and the Western Isles. The regions will range in size from the Borders (98,000 population) to Strathclyde (a mammoth region stretching from South Lanarkshire through Clydeside to the Island of Mull and containing some 2.5 million people). Similarly the districts will vary from sparsely populated, predominantly hill and moorland areas to districts comprised of the former cities, with populations ranging from 9,000 in the Badenoch and Strathspey District in the

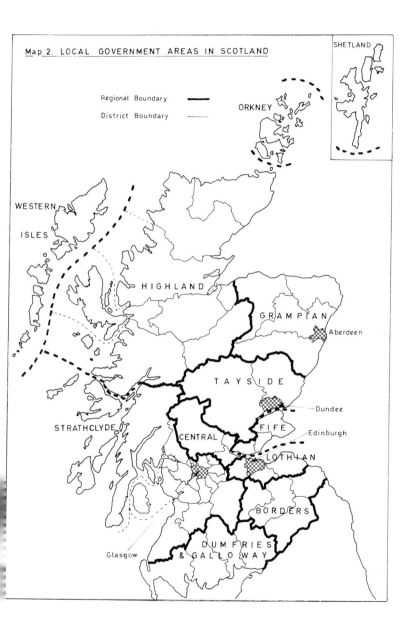

Map 2. LOCAL GOVERNMENT AREAS IN SCOTLAND

SHETLAND

Regional Boundary

District Boundary

ORKNEY

WESTERN

ISLES

HIGHLAND

GRAMPIAN

Aberdeen

TAYSIDE

Dundee

STRATHCLYDE

CENTRAL

FIFE

Edinburgh

LOTHIAN

BORDERS

Glasgow

DUMFRIES
& GALLOWAY

Highland region to 980,000 people in the Glasgow District of Strathclyde.[13]

Rural planning

The regional authorities will have wide-ranging responsibilities relating to rural and regional planning and development. They will be responsible for strategic planning matters, including the preparation of structure plans under the Town and Country Planning (Scotland) Act 1972. Three of the regional authorities – the Highland, Borders, and Dumfries and Galloway regions – will also be responsible for the preparation of local plans and the administration of development control. In other regions on the mainland these latter planning functions will be discharged by the district councils. All regional authorities will have responsibilities for industrial development, for roads and for public transport. They will also be concerned with various matters relating to tourism and recreation, to parks and to the countryside. This last group of functions will be exercised concurrently with the district councils. Clearly the new regional councils will be in a position to have a considerable influence over a wide range of rural development matters. I suggest, however, that if they are to succeed in discharging rural development responsibilities they will need, on the one hand, to have the kind of powers and financial discretion which are presently available to the Highlands and Islands Development Board and, on the other hand, they will need to adopt a more positive approach to rural affairs generally than has hitherto characterised the work of many planning departments.

Quite apart from rural development, if regional government in Scotland is to mean anything other than just bigger but not necessarily better, there must be more independence from central government, which means that the regional authorities must have a greater freedom over their expenditure. This raises many difficult issues concerned with local government finance, issues which were unfortunately excluded from the terms of reference of the Royal Commissions on Local Government. Somehow the regions must be given the opportunity to have a greater say over the kind of economy and indeed over the kind of society which they wish to develop and foster within their boundaries. For many regions this implies fundamental changes in relation to rural planning and development.

The statutory framework for planning in the countryside is provided by the Town and Country Planning Acts, supplemented by a variety of other measures such as the Countryside Acts, all of which have been framed primarily to suit urban conditions and to meet the needs of the urban population. The practice of planning in many rural parts of Britain has been essentially an urban type of planning – the operation of development control to preserve the character of villages, the control of advertisements, and more recently the provision of country parks, and so on. All these planning functions are important and it should be stressed that they have made a most important contribution to the countryside as we know it today. Nevertheless these activities are essentially urban in concept, as indeed is a very large part of the conservation movement which reflects urban needs and urban anxieties rather than necessarily the views of the people who live and work in the countryside. There are some people who would like to extend the same style of planning to a wider range of rural activities, for instance by bringing all new farm buildings and all afforestation under development control, but is this kind of extension of authority sufficient? Is it even desirable on its own?

It must be acknowledged that the real rural planning power at the present time, that is to say the taking of decisions which seriously affect the major land users, lies in the hands not of local planning authorities nor even of the central government departments concerned with town and country planning, but in the hands of the Agriculture Ministers and the Chancellor of the Exchequer. Scottish agriculture is influenced not by decisions taken by a group of local councillors but by the implementation of central government policies relating, for example, to improvement grants or subsidies for certain agricultural products. It is, I think, worthy of comment that when, in 1972, officers of the Department of Agriculture and Fisheries for Scotland were giving evidence before the House of Commons Select Committee on Scottish Affairs, it was stated that the Department has no direct rural planning responsibilities; its responsibilities relate only to questions of food production.[14] Civil servants may find such a separation of responsibilities easy to perceive, but it is surely in the interests of the Scottish countryside that somebody somewhere should see that food production cannot be separated from the many other uses of the countryside and from questions to do with the appearance and the economy of rural Scotland. As for forestry,

85

the other main rural land user, undoubtedly the most important factor leading to the afforestation of bare land within the private sector of the forestry industry is the system of income tax concessions which make it possible for an individual to establish a plantation at a low real cost, by offsetting the costs of establishment against taxable income from other sources, and to receive a virtually tax-free income on the sale of the timber. The tax concession has been operated in such a way as to encourage the blanket planting of conifers and the harvesting of woods by a clear felling system.

Regional Forest Policy

Forestry, I suggest, provides a good example of the scope for the devolution of greater responsibility from central government to the new regional authorities. In recent years there has been a marked shift of emphasis in national forest policy from what was originally a policy based predominantly on strategic considerations to a policy which retains production of timber as cheaply as possible as its main element, but which recognises the potential contribution of forestry as a source of employment in rural areas, as an influence on the appearance of the landscape and as a setting for recreation.[15] These newer policy elements are in my view much more appropriate for implementation at a regional level than on a national basis. They overlap with many of the responsibilities of regional authorities to which I have already referred; the new development plan system affords scope for a statement on forestry and forest policy to be included in structure plans. One might expect the regions of Scotland to have differing views on the future role of forestry (both state and private) within their areas. If, however, assistance to the private sector continues to be administered on a national basis, albeit to some extent on the advice of the Forestry Commission's Regional Committees, and the present system of tax concessions relating to commercial woodlands and timber is retained, it is difficult to see how the desirable flexibility in the pattern of forestry between regions can be achieved.

Consider briefly the Dumfries and Galloway region, covering a large area in the south west of Scotland with a population of only some 140,000. The region already contains extensive Forestry Commission plantations, including part of the well-known Glen

Trool Forest Park; there is in the region a stronger tradition of commercial forest management in the private sector than in most other parts of Britain, and, more recently, a sizeable acreage has been planted and is managed on behalf of the members of various forestry syndicates. In both state and private forests provision for public recreation has already been made in a variety of ways, but the region may anticipate a very marked increase in numbers of visitors over the next few years. In some parts of the region severe pressures from tourists have already been experienced and not long ago, for example, a local branch of the National Farmers Union of Scotland approached the Countryside Commission for Scotland for assistance in coping with the influx of visitors. If the region's forests are to play their appropriate role in relation to the provision of facilities for recreation, and in other respects, cooperation between the regional council, the Forestry Commission and representatives of the private sector of forestry is clearly vital. Everyone, or nearly everyone, accepts this, but the crucial question is to what extent such cooperation should be on an entirely voluntary basis or to what extent it should take place within a new framework of regional responsibility for the implementation of forest policy.

What size of forestry activity in the region is appropriate? What should be the extent of new planting? What are the needs of the producers for wood processing industries in association with the forests? Where should new processing industries be located? What kind of assistance to the private sector would be best suited to the needs of the region? What kind of recreation strategy for the woods as a whole would meet the needs of the region and would be complementary to the other elements of the regional and district councils' recreation policies? Questions such as these are primarily matters of regional concern and a blanket, inflexible, nationally-administered system of grant aid to forestry is inappropriate. It is not always in the interests of the landscape that a certain percentage of hardwoods should be included in any new plantation. It is not necessarily appropriate for recreation facilities to be provided where one landowner, including the Forestry Commission, thinks it might be a good or a profitable idea. Not every desirable project in the private sector is best assisted by a capital grant – the more important need may be for, say, a maintainance grant or some help from the local authority in such matters as the provision of an adequate system of wardens. The

87

answers to this kind of question in Dumfries and Galloway will not necessarily be appropriate for the Grampian region in the north east.

The need is for flexibility both between and within regions. The review of national forest policy over the last two or three years has, on present evidence, hardly begun to open the way for this kind of flexibility and is quite inadequate as a basis for the kind of forest policy which the Scottish regional authorities should be thinking about.[16] If the new authorities were to be given more positive powers of assistance in relation to forestry and were to seek constructively the cooperation of all forestry interests in their area, then thoughts of a mere extension of development control powers would fade into an appropriate perspective. If the regional authorities get only powers of control, this will be a recipe for disaster. It is to the advantage of all concerned that the experience and knowledge of the Forestry Commission and private sector of the industry should be harmonised with the interests of each region. No doubt, given goodwill, a certain amount can be achieved by informal consultative machinery established by agreement between the local authority and representatives from the forestry side, but it seems much more appropriate that consideration of forest policy, with all the possible implications for the economic and social life of the region, should take place within and not outside the framework of the duly elected local government system.

Conclusion

In conclusion, then, I suggest that the new regional councils should be the main agencies for rural development in Scotland. This requires, firstly, a greater understanding of rural affairs and a more positive approach towards rural land-using activities; secondly, greater financial independence from central government; and thirdly (and the first two must come first), more power to be devolved from central government upon the new authorities. In the absence of these changes the new Scottish regional authorities have little chance of succeeding as agencies for rural or any other kind of development in the 1980s and beyond.

*This paper attempts to describe the situation which existed in 1974, when it was first presented. Among relevant changes since then, apart from the anticipated re-organisation of local government in Scotland, are adjustments to the H.I.D.B. boundaries (partly to take account of the new local government areas) and very rapid growth of oil-related developments.

REFERENCES

1. Development Commissioners, *Change and Development in Rural Areas*, Thirty-third Report, H.M.S.O., London 1974.
2. Collier, A., *The Crofting Problem*, Cambridge University Press, 1953.
3. *Ibid*.
4. Grieve, R., 'Infrastructure in the Planning Process', *Town and Country Planning School, September 1972, Report of Proceedings*, Royal Town Planning Institute, London 1972.
5. Highlands and Islands Development Board, *Annual Reports*, H.I.D.B., Inverness, especially First (1966) and Seventh (1972).
6. Highlands and Islands Development Board, *North 7*, H.I.D.B., Inverness, occasional publication, esp. Nos. 16 and 17, 1973.
7. Russell, W., *In Great Waters*, Report on a study of the economic and social impact of the Highlands and Islands Development Board's investment in fisheries, Special Report 7, H.I.D.B., Inverness 1972.
8. Forestry Commission, *Annual Reports*, H.M.S.O., London.
9. Highlands and Islands Development Board, *Tourism in the Highlands and Islands*, H.I.D.B., Inverness, February 1974.
10. Jack Holmes Planning Group, *Moray Firth : A Plan for Growth*, H.I.D.B., Inverness 1968.
11. Oil Development Council for Scotland, *North Sea Oil and the Environment*, Report to the Oil Development Council by the Committee on the Environment, H.M.S.O., Edinburgh 1974.
12. Department of Energy, *Production and Reserves of Oil and Gas in the United Kingdom*, A report to Parliament by the Secretary of State for Energy, H.M.S.O., London 1974.
13. Planning Exchange, *The New Structure of Local Government in Scotland*, Newsheet 1, The Planning Exchange, Glasgow 1974.
14. House of Commons Select Committee on Scottish Affairs, *Minutes of Evidence*, Sub-Committee A, Tuesday 13th June 1972, Department of Agriculture and Fisheries for Scotland, H.C. Paper 51-XX, Session 1971-72, H.M.S.O., London 1972.
15. Forestry Commission, *op. cit.*; Ministry of Agriculture, Forestry and Food *et al.*, *Forestry Policy*, H.M.S.O., London 1972.
16. *Ibid*.

Regional and Rural Development

7. Development in Mid-Wales, 1957-73

D. P. GARBETT-EDWARDS

Over a period of sixteen years – from 1957 until 1973 – Local and Central Government cooperated in an attempt to encourage the development of the central rural region of Wales now known as Mid-Wales.

The region is one comprised of the 'old' counties (now the 'new' Districts) of Cardiganshire, Merioneth, Montgomeryshire and Radnorshire, together with the northern and rural parts of Breconshire. It is an area of some 3,000 sq. miles in which, at the time of the 1971 Census of Population, there was a population of 174,604. Over half the area's population lives in small villages and hamlets and isolated farmsteads. The remainder of the population lives in twenty-one regional centres which range from Aberystwyth with a population of over 10,000 to New Quay with a population of under 1,000. Several of these regional centres have extensive spheres of influence which cover as much as a third of the area of their parent counties.

For over a century Mid-Wales has suffered from depopulation – which, by generally accepted definition, is 'a substantial continuing decline in population'. It may be the result of net outward migration of sufficient volume to offset natural increase, but in extreme cases it can result from a combination of natural decrease and net outward migration.

Since 1871, when it was at its peak, Mid-Wales' population has fallen by over 100,000; since 1901 it has fallen by over 42,000. To appreciate its severity, this decline should be measured against the 1971 population of Montgomeryshire (43,119), Merioneth (35,330), or Radnorshire (18,279) (Table 1). The significance of the loss is only fully apparent, perhaps, when it is remembered that, whilst between 1901-71 Mid-Wales lost 19 per cent of its population, Wales as a whole showed an increase of 36 per cent.

Table 1: Population Changes in Mid-Wales 1901-71

Area	1901	1911	1921	1931	1951	1961	1971
Mid-Wales Industrial Development Association Area	217,277	208,542	208,382	194,003	185,729	178,546	174,604
Merioneth	48,852	45,565	45,087	43,201	41,465	38,310	35,330
Montgomeryshire	54,901	53,146	51,263	48,473	45,990	44,165	43,119
Cardiganshire	61,078	59,879	60,881	55,184	53,278	53,648	54,882
Radnorshire	23,281	22,590	23,517	21,323	19,993	18,471	18,279
North Breconshire	29,165	27,362	27,634	25,822	25,003	23,952	22,994

Source: Census of Population.

The bare facts of Mid-Wales' demographic trends do not of course disclose the composition of the areas population movement. Between 1961-71, 27 of the area's 43 County Districts lost population. Of the 23 Borough and Urban Districts, 12 lost population: of the 20 Rural Districts, 15 showed a loss. But, in fact, the Boroughs and Urban Districts collectively showed an overall increase of population – the region's net loss being accounted for by the loss from the rural areas.

Between 1901 and 1951, Mid-Wales lost an average of 640 people per year. Between 1951-61, the rate of loss increased to 718 per year. During the period 1961-71, the annual average rate of loss was reduced to 394.

Depopulation is generally referred to as the problem of Mid-Wales. It is not in fact *the* problem of Mid-Wales but the manifestation of a whole range of economic and social problems. These problems have been identified and examined in several reports of which the Beacham Report 'Depopulation in Mid-Wales' (H.M.S.O., 1964) was the forerunner.

The rapidly changing pattern of agriculture; the decline of employment in the extractive industries and other long-standing forms of employment; the low level of incomes; the inadequacy of the area's housing and the outdated settlement pattern of small and scattered towns and villages, are amongst the problems which show themselves ultimately in depopulation.

In the end, of course, depopulation is self-generating. The problems it creates create more problems. There is selective migration. The quality of local government suffers. A situation arises, too simply described perhaps, as 'no people – no jobs : no jobs – no people'. It was from this vicious circle of decline that in 1957 the area's Local Authorities sought to escape by forming the Mid-Wales Industrial Development Association. It was the purpose of the Association to stem the area's depopulation by encouraging the provision of new and diverse employment in manufacturing industry. The Association was guided by a Council comprised of three elected representatives and the Clerk from each of its five Constituent County Councils. It had an independent Chairman (Professor Arthur Beacham – 1957-63, and Mr Llevelys Davies – 1963-73) and its own small staff. It reported to the counties annually – but was otherwise given complete independence to act on their behalf. Its finance came from the counties themselves and from the Development Commission.

To some extent the establishment of the Association by the area's five County Councils, as they then were, was an act of practical protest against years of apparent disinterest and inaction by Government on the problems of Rural Wales. Government location of industry policy in the post-war years had focussed on the depressed areas of high unemployment and, despite the fact that because of depopulation their own social and economic problems were severe, the rural areas were ignored.

The Association itself decided to concentrate almost exclusively on the attraction of manufacturing industry. It did so for two reasons – firstly, because manufacturing wages were necessary to raise the very low level of incomes in the area and, secondly, because it saw no major developments – in terms of the provision of jobs – coming from the area's basic industries which were (and still are) agriculture, forestry and tourism.

In the event, the Association's policy appears to have been fully justified for throughout the 1961-71 period there was a massive decrease in all the basic sources of employment in Mid-Wales.

Agriculture	– 2233	– 49 per cent
Forestry	– 669	– 45 per cent
Quarrying	– 669	– 63 per cent
Transport	– 1212	– 66 per cent
Construction	– 1909	– 30 per cent

The pattern of agricultural change in Mid-Wales is no different from that experienced in similar areas. The trend towards the bigger farm unit, mechanisation and technical advance all contribute to the decline in the number of employees who find their work on the land. In regard to Forestry, Mid-Wales with its high rainfall and marginal uplands remains an excellent growing area – but increased productivity has allowed a reduction in the full-time labour force employed in the forests.

In neither case have the commercial attractions of processing the area's timber or some of the products of its agriculture been sufficient to outweigh the problems of establishing such enterprises in Mid-Wales.

Tourism is an essential basic industry of Mid-Wales. The area with its beautiful countryside and ample space has obviously a considerable tourist potential. Its continued development will do

Mid-Wales nothing but good. But in the end, the effect which the development of tourism will have on depopulation will depend on its capacity to generate employment and incomes. Whether it can make any major contribution in this respect remains to be seen.

The Association's efforts to attract new industry to Mid-Wales had to be made against a situation where, largely as a result of years of depopulation, there was no heavy unemployment and, except for isolated pockets, no large pools of labour to which incoming firms could be attracted. Similarly, as a consequence of past decline, the area as a whole had little more than 2,500 school leavers annually and half of them were already committed to agriculture or to some form of advanced education. The remaining reservoir of school leavers was hardly sufficient to meet the needs of existing industry and commerce, let alone to service new developments.

Furthermore the traditions of the area lay in academic education – and education which in the past had provided the best means of escape from the poverty (in respect of both finance and opportunity) of the rural Welsh background. Industrial employment was unknown in many parts of Mid-Wales. Moreover, the area had become so used to its brightest elements migrating, that it had begun to equate migration with success and to consider that those who chose to remain could not be quite with it!

After three years of fact-finding and planning the Association itself began to move forward to positive results in the early 1960s. As it had expected, it found that there was in Mid-Wales a reservoir of hidden unemployed – particularly female – that there was a good deal of underemployment and that, given the opportunity, a proportion of the area's school leavers *were* interested in remaining in the area to take up new industrial employment. Additionally, the Association found there was a small but steady stream of labour coming from agriculture and other sources. It found also that, against the background of competition for labour in the conurbations which applied even in that period, industry *could* be interested in establishing in Mid-Wales to utilise the labour which was and which would be available.

The Association rapidly became – and remained – the spearhead of the Local Authorities efforts to attract new industry to Mid-Wales. Its success depended not only upon its own expertise in publicising the area and in promoting its development, but also upon the support it received from the authorities in providing the sites and services which incoming firms required. Whilst the goodwill of the authorities (five counties and 43 districts!) was never in question, the lack of financial resources and, sometimes, of a *real* commitment by authorities to the development of their particular areas, caused problems in the provision of the facilities necessary to industrial development. Nevertheless, given time, all the authorities responded.

It is a matter of fact that when the Association began its work very little land had been allocated for industry in any of the County Development Plans. Some land had been allocated in Blaenau Ffestiniog, Welshpool and in mid-Cardiganshire but such allocation was entirely inadequate. Initially small areas of an acre or two were allocated as and when a factory was attracted to the region. Ultimately, proper allocations were made of sites ranging from five to 25 acres in all the Mid-Wales towns. Towards the end of the 1960s, despite the financial burden involved, several authorities acquired and developed small industrial estates, even going so far as to provide access roads and main services. Indeed as might be expected, it was in those areas such as Brecon, Corwen, Rhayader and Welshpool, where the Local Authorities did most to support the attraction of industry by developing their own industrial estates, that the best results were achieved.

Whilst it was for Local Government to provide the facilities for incoming industry, the success of industrial development in Mid-Wales depended much upon the attitude of and support from Central Government. When the Association started its work, no Government assistance of any kind was available to encourage the establishment of industry in Mid-Wales. However, one of the Association's first approaches was to the Development Commission – an arm of Government which (operating under the terms of the Development and Road Improvements Funds Act 1909 and 1910) has a particular responsibility for maintaining the well-being of the rural areas of the United Kingdom.

Although the Development Commission had not previously been directly concerned with the establishment of industry in the countryside as a means of stemming depopulation, it responded to the Association's approach and agreed to finance the building of factories which might be let on attractive 'market-value' terms to firms establishing in Mid-Wales.

The partnership established between the Mid-Wales Industrial

Development Association and the Development Commission in the 1960s undoubtedly laid the basis for the more rapid development which the region was later to achieve.

Initially the Commission agreed only to finance 'purpose-built' factories for firms which were prepared to commit themselves to development in the area prior to the factory being constructed. The first such factory built in 1959 was, in fact, not a new factory at all – but the renovation and extension of a disused school in Machynlleth for use by a clothing firm. This factory, which has since been enlarged and is still operating, was the forerunner of many more factories which the Commission was to build.

In its early years, the Association found (what now seems to be obvious!) that industrialists could be more readily attracted to Mid-Wales if they could be offered factories – ready and waiting – rather than green-field sites however pleasant. It was, then, in 1964 that the next major advance came in Mid-Wales when the Association applied successfully to the Development Commission for the building of 'advance' factories in the area. These were, as their name implies, factories built in advance of specific demand. Not only did these factories provide a new impetus to industrial development in the region but, by the fact that they were built in locations pre-determined by the Association, they were used very much as an *instrument* of the area's regional development policy.

The grounds on which the Development Commission provided the finance for the building of factories in Mid-Wales was that the employment provided by each unit would make a substantial contribution to stemming depopulation in the area in which its factory was built. It was for the Association, as the regional organisation, to make the 'case' for the building of each factory. The cases made by the Association were fully documented and the facts of the area's depopulation were clearly established. Gradually the need for a solution to the area's problems won acceptance. In 1966 the Government broadened its industrial location policy by agreeing that population change, including migration, should be one of the criteria for establishing an area as a Development Area. This change of policy owed much to the case which the Association had made over the years for action on the problems of Mid-Wales.

Mid-Wales was scheduled as a Development Area in 1966 and subsequently a wide range of financial assistance from the Government has been available to firms establishing in the area. From the time when Mid-Wales was scheduled as a Development

Area, the pace and scale of the area's industrial development increased substantially.

Within the limits of the modest resources it had available, the Association actively publicised and promoted Mid-Wales as an attractive location for industrial development. The major part of its publicity was through direct mail advertising backed by suitable advertising in the national, provincial and local press and in trade and business journals. It published and widely circulated many different booklets on the facilities which the area offered for development. Throughout, the Association pursued an active press and public relations policy.

The pattern of new industrial development in Mid-Wales in the period 1957-1973 is as follows:

Factories occupied

New privately-built factories		23	
Government-financed factories			
purpose-built factories	12		
advance factories	11		
nursery factories	4	27	
existing factories		3	
premises adapted to industrial use		11	
Mid-Wales Development Corporation, Newtown			
advance factories	8		
purpose-built factory	1		
nursery factories	10	19	83

Factories available

Government-financed factories	
advance factories	3

Factories under construction

Government-financed factories			
advance factories	2		
nusery factories	8	10	
Mid-Wales Development Corporation, Newtown			
advance factories	4		
mini factories	8	12	22
			108

(as at 30th September 1973)

During the period 1957-73, in which the Association was working, 83 new factories opened in Mid-Wales. (In addition, at 30th September 1973 there were three advance factories available for occupation and six advance factories and 16 nursery factories were in the course of construction). The area's 83 new factories were operated by 76 firms – some firms having more than one factory. The introduction of these new industries more than doubled the number of industries which were operating in Mid-Wales when the Association was formed in 1957. At the end of 1973 there were 126 manufacturing industries in the area employing ten or more people.

The 71 Government-financed factories given in the above table provide a floor area of some 650,000 sq. ft and represent a public investment in Mid-Wales to the order of £3 million. The building of the factories has been carried out by the Development Commission, the Department of Trade (which now builds the area's purpose-built factories and provides advance factories in Mid-Wales' few areas of severe unemployment) and by the Mid-Wales Development Corporation which is responsible for the development of Mid-Wales' first new town at Newtown. Building of the factories has been shared as follows:

Advance factories

Development Commission	14	
Department of Trade	2	
Mid-Wales Development Corporation	12	28

Purpose-built factories

Development Commission	9	
Department of Trade	3	
Mid-Wales Development Corporation	1	13

Nursery factories

Development Commission	12	
Mid-Wales Development Corporation	18	30

(as at 30th September 1973).

Clothing and engineering firms predominate amongst the new firms which have established in the area – but in addition to these groups the range of products of the area's new firms is now extensive; it varies from office filing equipment, push-chairs, packaging, leathercloth and hydraulic seals to enamel kitchenware, fishing tackle, surgical sutures, plastic bottles and carpet yarn.

The new firms themselves range from internationally-known companies such as G.K.N., Vickers, Dowty's, Tootal and Slimma to other well-established public and private companies and to smaller new companies setting up in business for the first time.

With the exception of nursery factories of 1500 sq. ft and mini factories of 3000 sq. ft the new factories which were built in Mid-Wales between 1957 and 1973 varied from units of 4500 sq. ft to 100,000 sq. ft. The standard unit was of 10,000 sq. ft. On average the factories each provided employment for 50 people, with actual employment ranging from five to 500.

A comparison of Department of Employment's statistics of employed population in Mid-Wales at June 1961 and 1971 shows an increase of 3,533 (+ 83 per cent) in the number of people employed in Mid-Wales' manufacturing industries. In mid-1971 there were 7,765 people employed in the area's manufacturing industries. The changing pattern of the area's employment is plainly to be seen in the fact that, although Mid-Wales is thought of as an agricultural area, at mid-1971 for every one person employed (but not *self*-employed) in the area's agriculture there were three people employed in the area's manufacturing industries.

During the decade 1961-71, when much of this new industrial development took place, there appeared for the first time for many years signs of a slackening in the area's depopulation. Between 1951-61 the population of Mid-Wales declined by 7,183 (–3.9 per cent): in the ten years 1961-71, the area's population loss was reduced to 3,942 (–2.2 per cent).

From the outset it was the Association's aim to be an essentially practical organisation which would achieve its object of stemming depopulation by positive results in 'attracting new industry'. Yet very soon in its work the Association found that the area's industrial development and its general development were inextricably linked and that it was virtually impossible to be concerned with one without the other. At its most simple, factories needed people, people needed houses, houses needed services and so on... Similarly in respect of policy, the Association found it impossible to be concerned with the policy of industrial development in the countryside without being concerned with the general policy objectives of such development. What sort of countryside, what sort of economy, what sort of settlement pattern, what sort of rural society was it intended to create?

The Association had, from the outset, recognised that the existing settlement pattern of Mid-Wales was in itself a fundamental cause of depopulation. Based on a nineteenth-century agriculture and means of transport, the settlement pattern of small and scattered towns and villages created immense difficulties in the provision of public services, educational facilities, public transport, hospital services, and so on. The thin spread of population made it difficult to gather together a labour force of any great size in any one place. The provision of public services for so small and scattered a population was generally uneconomic. In human terms the settlement pattern inhibited social organisation at a standard demanded in the present day.

Initially, in the absence of any guidelines to development, the area concentrated closely on its objective of 'stemming depopulation'. To achieve such an objective meant that there must be a fairly widespread distribution of industry – aimed at plugging the drain of population at its source. Yet to distribute industry in this way could only result in maintaining the existing settlement pattern and keeping things as they were – when it was for the very reason that things were as they were (too few people, too scattered, a society too expensive and inhibitive of modern standards of social organisation) that the area was depopulating in the first place!

Throughout the early 1960s careful consideration was given by the Association to the need for concentration of development and to the gradual re-shaping of the settlement pattern to one which would meet the needs of a twentieth-century economy. Alongside these policy considerations, the Association's practical experience in attracting industry was showing that the area simply did not have enough people to generate development on the scale necessary to make an impact on the problem which it was intended to solve. Despite the encouraging results which had been achieved in attracting new industry, it was the Association's view that with 174,000 people spread over 3,000 sq. miles, the population of Mid-Wales was too sparse and too scattered to allow the introduction of industry at the speed and scale necessary to revitalize its economy and stem its depopulation.

The Association saw the solution to depopulation lying in the repopulation of the area. Repopulation meaning the attraction of 'new' population to the region and, as new employment grew, the retention of more and more of the area's own people. It meant also the re-shaping and strengthening of the existing settlement pattern through the concentration of major growth in a relatively few towns and villages.

In the late 1960s and early 1970s Mid-Wales took its first steps towards the implementation of this policy. Firstly, in re-shaping the settlement pattern it evolved a 'growth town' strategy which won Government acceptance. It was agreed that except in cases of special need, all the Government's speculative factory building aimed at attracting industry would be concentrated in seven towns.Clearly the intention was not to overwhelm these towns with industrial development, but to stimulate their growth into bigger and 'better' places in which more people will want to live and be able to work.

The towns selected were Aberystwyth, Bala, Brecon, Llandrindod Wells, Rhayader, Welshpool and Newtown. They are located on the main north/south and east/west roads in Mid-Wales and are so situated that the majority of the region's existing population is within 20 miles travel-to-work of the new employment which these seven towns will have to offer.

Secondly, Mid-Wales also began the attempt to attract 'new' population to the region. For many years consideration had been given to the establishment of a New Town in Mid-Wales. The Association itself advocated such a project as far back as 1959 – but it was not until 1965 that the Government commissioned a feasibility study into the building of a new town for 70,000 people at Caersws. Although the scheme had a great deal to commend it, the Government decided instead to proceed with its plans for development in Mid-Wales by expanding Newtown, Montgomeryshire. The Mid-Wales Development Corporation was set up in 1968 under New Towns Act powers to expand Newtown from a population of 5,000 to 11,500 by the early 1980s. Even at the time of the Corporation's establishment it was said by the Government that the extension of its remit to other towns in Mid-Wales could be considered in the light of its success at Newtown.

The use of the New Towns Act as an instrument for rural regional development was an interesting and important experiment. At Newtown, with its own staff, finance and powers, the Mid-Wales Development Corporation made very rapid progress. It completed all the necessary statutory processes by 1970 and thereafter in four years built 300 houses (with another 500 in construction), 27 factories and a 50,000 sq. ft. office block. It constructed a £2 million sewerage scheme. Over 700 new jobs were provided in the town's new and existing industries and another 1,200 were in the pipeline. The population of the town increased by over 1,500 and there were the first signs of growth for many years in several surrounding villages.

Up to mid-1974, except at Newtown, the Government had not taken any special steps to implement the 'growth town' strategy to which it had given its approval. Whilst progress had been made with the preparation of plans and in one or two towns some small scale development had been achieved, left to their own insufficient human and financial resources the 'old' local authorities concerned had not been able to implement effectively the strategy on which their towns' expansion and the area's well-being so largely depended.

It was at Newtown that tangible evidence was provided of the impact which can be achieved in implementing a 'growth town' strategy if there is real intent and if adequate means and powers are provided to do the job.

The effort which the Association led on behalf of its constituent County Councils for 16 years from 1957-73, showed that with the combined assistance of local and central government, industry could be attracted to Mid-Wales. Income levels were raised. Morale improved. The region made a greater contribution to the national well-being. Depopulation was reduced. Through the new employment provided, a demand for people was created – and such a demand is fundamental to the solution of any region's depopulation. The Association identified the region's problems and by an empirical approach pointed to their solution.

Through what was a loose, entirely voluntary arrangement based on common cause and goodwill, the five former County Councils of Mid-Wales established through the Association a cohesive regional development policy. It is a policy on which, if they choose, the area's new local authorities and central Government can work together to create a prosperous rural region in which twenty-first-century people will want to live – and the area's problem of depopulation will finally be solved.

Regional and Rural Development

8. Regional Planning Strategies in France

I. B. THOMPSON

The French system of planned regional development has attracted much attention as a model of an elaborate machinery for intervention within a mixed economy. It would, however, be misleading to regard French experience as necessarily instructive in a British context, or to consider the methods as being transferable to the British setting. Major contrasts exist between the background to planning in the two countries. France is considerably larger, with correspondingly wider environmental, economic and social variations at a regional scale. There is also a much larger rural and agricultural sector, which has flavoured the motivation and character of planning in many of her regions. Regional planning in France, moreover, rests on a framework of state economic planning and within which it forms an instrument for intervention. Finally, France has enjoyed a prolonged period of economic growth sustained by high levels of investment. The planning structures which have evolved out of an expansionist background inevitably differ in emphasis from those generated in an atmosphere of low growth. This paper seeks to characterise French regional planning in a triple perspective; in terms of its motivation, the strategies employed and the ambiguities that remain unresolved.[1][2][3]

The motivation of planned regional development

French regional planning has followed a highly complex evolution from largely *ad hoc* policies stemming in part from spontaneous grass roots origins in the early 1950s, to the present elaborate apparatus. It follows that the motives underlying planning have not remained entirely constant, but have similarly evolved according to the changing political, economic and social imperatives of the past two decades. Nevertheless, five main motivations may be isolated as having been either of continuing importance or particular relevance at the present time.

The dominant motive both at present and throughout the evolution of regional planning, is the attempt to reduce severe regional disparities in the level of social and economic development. Specifically, a line drawn roughly from the estuary of the Seine to the Rhône delta defines a basic socio-economic cleavage between the eastern 'developed' third of the nation, and the western, central and south-western 'underdeveloped' two-thirds of the national space.[4] Whatever criteria are employed as indicators of levels of development, a consistent distinction emerges between these two zones. Seventy per cent of the urban population and almost the same proportion of the total population resides in the eastern third of the nation. In turn this reflects the overwhelming concentration of the nation's energy production, manufacturing capacity and advanced agricultural output, together with a correspondingly elaborate transport infrastructure, in the eastern zone. The scale of this disparity has long been regarded as excessive, the more so as spontaneous forces tend to perpetuate and even widen the gap. The external economies of access to a large market, diversified labour pool, superior infrastructures and a favourable demographic structure enjoyed by eastern France, contrast with the under-industrialised west, with inherent locational disadvantages, distorted demographic structure, deficient communications and retarded agriculture. The problem of regional disparity is not restricted to this simple east-west dichotomy, for superimposed on this is the gulf between the Paris region and the remainder of the country. Paris enjoys a quasi-monopoly of the power of decision in both public and private sectors, and has a disproportionate concentration of the nation's economic and cultural substance. As a consequence, the range and quality of opportunity, together with levels of remuneration, are much higher in the capital, with its agglomeration of nine million inhabitants, than elsewhere in France. A dual motivation for regional planning, therefore, has been a consistent attempt to reduce the level of disparity in development, opportunity and income as between eastern and western France, and simultaneously, to restrain the excessive dominance of Paris over the nation as a whole.

The crude division between east and west is an over-simplified distinction and certain planning problems have the reverse distribution. In particular, the problems of declining industries, urban decay, environmental pollution and traffic congestion affect especially the agglomerations of eastern France. A second motivation of planned regional development is thus the attempt to renovate both the economy and urban environment of a limited number of old industrial areas located in eastern France. The prime examples are the industrialised coal basins of the Nord and Saint Etienne, the textiles conurbation of Lille-Roubaix-Tourcoing, the metallurgical districts of Lorraine and the Ardennes, and a scattering of small coalfields on the fringe of the Massif Central. In these instances, the decline of coal or ore extraction is accompanied by a rationalisation of associated staple industries, leading to declining employment opportunities both for displaced workers and the new generation of school and university leavers. At the same time, a revived industrial basis is needed as a springboard for overdue programmes of urban renewal.

The first two motivations apply to readily discernible situations, easily transferable into quantified terms, as numbers of new jobs required, targets for housing construction, necessary increase in income levels and other such concrete aims and priorities. A third motivation has a more technical character and is a matter of organisation rather than the achievement of specific development goals, at least in the first instance. France has embarked on a number of ambitious regional development projects which demand an integrated approach to resource use over large areas, and thus a regional field of action. These projects commonly involve entire physical units, for example drainage basins, lowland plains or coastal tracts, which seldom correspond with existing administrative units and usually span a number of *départements* and local authority boundaries. The need for integrated resource management implies a close degree of collaboration at local authority level within an overall development strategy. The prime example is the integrated development of the Rhône valley, involving electricity generation, flood control, irrigation, improved navigation and industrial location. Similar situations have arisen in Languedoc, Corsica and the Durance valley. An important motivation of planning has thus been the need to create appropriate institutional structures at a regional scale, to initiate and execute programmes of resource development and management.

A similar set of circumstances, in the sense of a need for coordinated development, explains a fourth motivation for planned intervention; the need to structure the development of metropolitan regions. The most outstanding case is that of the Paris region, but a limited number of provincial agglomerations have also reached a stage of metropolitan growth culminating in the existence of city regions polarised by a strong central node or urban complex. In the past, such agglomerations have grown in anarchic fashion with a poor adjustment between the administrative framework and the functional realities of the urban system. The need to plan on a metropolitan scale in order to structure the growth of rapidly evolving city regions is now recognised, and marries on the one hand strategic decisions on employment growth, housing targets and amenity provision, with, on the other, the preparation of physical plans to direct and accommodate future growth.

A final motivation, at present only hesitantly expressed, has come in the wake of the E.E.C., and is political in character. The avowed objective of closer economic integration throws into relief the existence of weak regions as obstacles to fuller international integration. Such weaker regions commonly coincide with a peripheral location relative to the core areas of the Market. It is difficult to envisage an integrated E.E.C. while there is a lack of effective integration within the component nations. Secondly, the move towards fuller integration calls upon the frontier regions, like the Nord and Alsace, to play an international role, with coordinated planning decisions taken across political boundaries.

The strategies of planned regional development

In spite of its relationship to the national plans, French regional planning does not consist of a single monolithic administrative structure. In effect, regional planning is an omnibus term for a wide range of administrative organs, institutional bodies, departmental policies emanating from various ministries, the activities of regional development corporations and long-range strategic planning agencies. A very complex aggregate has thus grown up over a 20 year period but within which some six main strands may be differentiated as being of particular importance.

The excessive centralisation of administration, and the resultant concentration of all meaningful decision-making in Paris, has led to a growing demand from the regions for greater decentralisation. The strength of this demand varies regionally, but is strongest in those regions with a distinctive cultural and historical unity, especially where this coincides, as in Brittany and Corsica, for example, with charges of past neglect by the central government. In these circumstances there is a movement for some degree of regional autonomy. More commonly, the pressure has been simply for a greater devolution of administration to the provinces, accompanied by a desire for greater regional participation in decision-making. In response to these pressures, successive governments have engaged on a strategy of 'regionalisation' which is becoming of increasing importance as a planning framework. Until 1972 the regionalisation strategy involved two elements; the setting up of administrative organs at a regional level, and the recognition of previously unofficial 'regional expansion committees' as having an advisory and consultative role. In 1960, the country was divided into 21 (subsequently 22) regions as a basis for harmonisation of the principal State-controlled institutions. The regions thus emerged as administrative units, headed by a Regional Prefect directly responsible to the central government. The essential function in planning terms thus became the translation of the objectives and priorities established in the National Plans into action at the regional level. Some degree of initiative was invested in the regional level through the constitution of Regional Economic Development Commissions (C.O.D.E.R.) in 1964, consisting of experts and representatives of regional interests. As with the former regional committees, their role remained a purely consultative one. In practice, the measure of devolution achieved by the reforms of the early 1960s was small, since the central government retained control of policy-making and the allocation of funds for regional development, but at least a machinery existed at regional level to administer and execute planning decisions made and financed by central government. In 1972, 'regionalisation' was taken a stage further by major legislation on regional reform. While retaining the same regional subdivisions, the reform provided for the creation of Regional Councils. These are composed of the elected deputies and senators, together with representatives of the elected members of local government. These councils have enlarged executive powers on matters of regional development, together with powers to raise financial resources to promote regional development and to complement the funds allocated for this purpose by central government. In addition, the former C.O.D.E.R. are replaced by Economic and Social Committees reflecting the various regional interests but still retaining a purely advisory function.

This new regional administrative system is only now becoming operational and it would be premature to pass judgment. It is appropriate to note, however, that the composition of the Regional Councils inevitably introduces a greater element of 'politicisation' into regional government and thus a potential element of stress, both internally and *vis à vis* the central government. Secondly, the retention of the much criticised regional divisions, with their great variations in size and population, may promote further anomalies. Since the capacity to raise development funds internally is a strict function of population size and economic strength, the reform may favour those populous regions which are already urbanised and industrialised as opposed to the weaker regions most in need of development. For all its deficiencies and ambiguities, France nevertheless does have a regional framework within which planning decisions can be taken and implemented and pressure brought to bear on the central government in favour of regional development.

A second strand in the spectrum of strategies invoked on behalf of regional development is that of regional policies exercised by the various government departments. This involves a myriad of policies emanating from, for example, the ministries of agriculture, transport, industry and manpower among others. The list of departmental policies with regional implications is extremely long, and a single example of a regional policy, as opposed to a formal regional plan, must suffice. State assistance to industrial development has become increasingly important in regional planning since the 1950s, initially to aid certain critical zones with high unemployment levels but progressively as a means of influencing the overall distribution of industry. A complex system of investment grants and fiscal exonerations now exists which favours new investment in two broad areas: the 'development zone' consisting of virtually the whole of western and central France, and the 'conversion zones' comprised of a scattering of industrial areas in eastern France which are undergoing a contraction of their basic activities. Government incentives thus promote industrialisation in response to two differing regional problems. On the one hand, new investment is required to raise the level of industrialisation throughout western France in order to increase opportunity, income levels and to compensate for declining employment in the overloaded agricultural sector. On the other hand, the run down of mining activity, which in some smaller coalfields amounts to total closure, the rationalisation of textiles manufacturing and the metallurgical industries, has created a need for diversification in some of the oldest established industrial areas of eastern France. Coupled with the preferential treatment of the above two zones is the attempt to restrict industrial development in the Paris region and thus to promote decentralisation of industry. The policy of intervention in industrial location has experienced elements of both success and failure. Initially, firms restricted from expanding in Paris were reluctant to move great distances and the result was the industrialisation of a large number of small and medium-sized towns within the Paris Basin. In effect this was a 'spontaneous' decentralisation since few of the movements qualified for substantial aid under the terms of locational incentives, which certainly aided the process of decongesting Paris but which did little to help the areas most seriously needing new industry. More recently some success has been achieved in terms of longer-range decentralisation and the creation of entirely new activities in the conversion zones. In the latter context the recent implantation of large units of the vehicle building industry on the Northern Coalfield is a striking development. On the other hand, the policy has not yet succeeded in attracting sufficient investment to the more peripheral regions, and particularly the south west, nor has Lorraine attracted enough new employment to offset the declining opportunities in ore mining and metallurgy. It is apparent too that the policy does not operate entirely in isolation from other factors. In the case of the nationalised industries and those in which the State is a major shareholder or customer, a considerable amount of government impulsion is involved. In addition, a significant factor in attracting investment to specific areas is the degree of initiative and enterprise shown by the regional authorities and interests themselves, as well as the amount of investment authorised and financed by the State in infrastructure development. In both these aspects, the recent success of the Nord region is instructive.

A third strand in planned regional development is that of prospective or long-range strategic planning. This grew out of the concern that the national plans, which, in the initial stages at least, were involved with establishing national targets and priorities, might neglect the regional implications inherent in the allocation of resources. It was further feared that the relatively short time span of the national plans, usually five years, would result in a lack of continuity in regional development. The Commission Nationale d'Aménagement du Territoire was therefore created in 1963 as a permanent commission within the national planning structure, to establish the long term perspective of planned regional development. At the same time the Délégation à l'Aménagement et à l'Action Régionale (D.A.T.A.R.) was created as a small but powerful body charged with the task of providing a coordinating and driving force to government regional policies. France was thus provided with a framework for projecting planning decisions into the future and a means of intervention at the regional level in development projects appropriate to these aims. As an example of long-range planning, the case may be cited of the policy of establishing 'métropoles d'équilibre', inaugurated in 1964. The policy of promoting the growth of eight regional metropolises was designed to create major provincial capitals capable of counter-balancing the excessive weight of Paris within their respective regions. At the same time the metropolises were intended to act as motivators of economic growth at a regional level. To these ends, priority investment was to be accorded not only for industrial development but also for major expansions of tertiary activities and of infrastructures. The policy received considerable criticism,[5] for whereas certain cities, notably Lyon, had a certain credibility as potential metropolises, others had neither the economic nor the cultural strength to fulfill this role. Some, like Lille, were arguably too close to Paris to escape its dominance, others were too close together, like Nancy and Strasbourg, or consisted of poorly integrated polycentric urban aggregates, like Nancy–Metz and Nantes–St Nazaire, lacking in metropolitan character. Other strong regional centres, as Rouen and Rennes were omitted altogether. Criticism was also levelled at the assumption that such metropolises, even with enhanced functions, would be capable of reanimating their tributary regions. There was an equal possibility that on the contrary they would drain their regions of population as a result of their increased status. Above all, it was difficult to imagine the new metropolises offering a credible counterweight to Paris while the power of decision, both in government and the private sector, remained the prerogative of Paris.

The policy of promoting 'métropoles d'équilibre' has now fallen virtually into abeyance and attention has been switched to the medium-sized towns, many of which are growing at more rapid rates than the nominated metropolises. Nevertheless, this example of prospective planning is of interest since it attempted to intervene in the hierarchy of French cities and to establish artificially a system previously governed by largely spontaneous forces. It is an example also of the pitfalls of long-range planning based on an empirical approach. This discussion is also relevant as an introduction to a fourth strand in the strategy of regional development, since the creation of metropolises was a stepping stone towards planning on a metropolitan scale.

A precedent for metropolitan planning was established with the publication of the P.A.D.O.G. proposals for the Paris agglomeration in 1960 and the subsequent Schéma Directeur for the Paris Region in 1965.[6] The well known Schéma Directeur is basically a structure plan involving the whole of the Paris agglomeration and the adjacent portions of the central Paris Basin which experience the direct impact of the national capital. The Schéma affords a blueprint for physical planning and thus for coordinated decision-making with respect to the location of new towns and suburban nodes, employment, transport facilities, the provision of services and preservation of amenities, guided by long-range strategies for the size and structure of the city region as a whole. This comprehensive view of metropolitan development was given an even wider setting in 1970 by the establishment of a Paris Basin planning unit, which aims to integrate future development throughout this huge area, and involves the preparation of structure plans for certain crucial urbanised zones. These include the 'support zones' of the Lower Seine valley, the Middle Loire and Oise–Aisne valleys, and northern Champagne, which are growing rapidly in response to decentralisation of activity from Paris.

From its origins in the Paris region, the practice of metropolitan structure planning was extended in 1966 to include the urbanised zones surrounding the nominated 'métropoles d'équilibre'. Metropolitan planning organisations (O.R.E.A.M.) were created charged with the task of preparing strategic plans, on the Paris model, indicating the future directions of growth, land use and infrastructure development. This recognised the need for integrated planning in the major agglomerations, hitherto frustrated by the fragmentation of the local government structure. Although such strategic plans are clearly subject to subsequent modification, particularly in the light of demographic trends, nevertheless, the elevation of physical planning from a local to a regional scale will be a force moulding the detail of regional development in the future.

A final strategy, which in some ways comes closest to pure regional planning, has been the creation of regional development companies, charged with specific objectives and usually organised on a mixed economy basis. Their activities may be regarded as 'pure' in the sense that they involve integrated resource management within rationally defined units, as opposed to *ad hoc* intervention in an arbitrary system of regions. Their mixed economy structure endows them with strong legal powers and financial backing emanating from the government while retaining some of the flexibility of private enterprise within which regional interests may be involved. The major precedent for this form of development was the Compagnie Nationale du Rhône, created before the last war to promote the integrated development of the Rhône valley and involving energy production, improved navigation and agricultural development. A similar blending of State involvement and private operation occurs in the Compagnie Nationale d'Aménagement du Bas-Rhône Languedoc, which since 1955 has been responsible for agricultural modernisation and rural renovation in the viticultural zone of the Languedoc plain.[7] Regional development in Corsica is vested in two companies, the S.O.M.I.V.A.C. responsible for land reclamation and agricultural resettlement, and the S.E.T.C.O. with responsibility for the promotion of tourism.[8] Similarly, the creation of ambitious new tourist complexes on the Languedoc coast, directed by an inter-ministerial mission, involved mixed economy development companies at the construction stage. In practice, the adoption of the mixed economy development company formula has proved appropriate in regions of chronic underdevelopment or maladjustment, where reliance on the private sector alone would have yielded results too slowly, or where infrastructure works requiring massive investment and strong legal powers made government participation inevitable. In spite of impressive results, the development companies have not escaped criticism. Although integrated internally, their external impact on other regions has not always been coordinated. Moreover, by absorbing large amounts of public money, with slow returns initially, they divert public investment from other regions with equally strong claims for preferential treatment. They have therefore tended to become sensitive politically, and developments on the scale of the Rhône and Languedoc are likely to decline in favour of less ambitious projects with a greater participation of private capital.

Ambiguities in planned regional development

The selection of six main strands for discussion has done scant justice to the complexity of French regional planning. Many important elements have been omitted, particularly under the heading of regional policies. Clearly, policies on agricultural reform, motorway construction and port expansion, for example, have profound significance in terms of regional growth. Similarly, the creation of regional and national parks, together with aid for recreation and tourism, affect the character of regional development in certain parts of France. Even the limited view presented in this brief paper does, however, serve to highlight certain ambiguities which are by no means confined to French experience.

The fundamental question may be asked as to whether formal regional planning does not produce self-defeating results, in the sense of highlighting the outstanding potential of certain regions, leading to ambitious plans, and the limited development potential of others. The idea that regional planning can bring about a 'levelling' process is not supported by the evidence from France. Rather does it indicate that the role of regional planning is to define the vocation of a given region – that is what it can achieve successfully, profitably and competitively – and then to give the maximum aid to fulfill that vocation. A second ambiguity surrounds the form of regional structure adopted as a planning basis. Although France has a framework of administrative regions on which certain planning decisions may be based, it has been found necessary to resort to additional regional strategies, with varying spatial extents. It is doubtful too whether all planning problems have a 'regional' context in the orthodox sense of standard planning regions. The case may be cited of 'axial' regions, corresponding with strong lines of communication, traversing several regions and even crossing international frontiers, which face common development problems throughout their extent, but do not conform to a formal regional framework.

A country as large as France also poses the question of how realistic decentralisation policies can be made. Concentration in economic activity has taken place for reasons of locational advantage. It is an unresolved question as to how far firms can be encouraged to move from the core area of eastern France without damaging their competitive position. This particularly affects the peripheral and terminal regions because, although improved transport links certainly reduce the locational disadvantage, at the same time they improve their accessibility as markets from existing centres of activity and thus reduce the incentive to relocate production. Finally, the experience of France demonstrates the advantages of a relationship between regional planning and planning at a national level. To take a very simple analogy, it is hard to fit in the pieces of a jigsaw without having the picture illustration as a guide.

REFERENCES

1. The structure of planned regional development in France is summarised in Monod, J., and Castelbajac, Ph. de, *L'Aménagement du Territoire*, Presses Universitaires de France, 1971.

2. A full discussion of French regional planning and an analysis of all the regions appears in Thompson I. B., *Modern France. A Social and Economic Geography*, Butterworths, 1970.

3. Individual themes within the planning sphere, together with regional case studies are discussed in Clout, H., *The Geography of Post-War France*, Pergamon, 1972.

4. Thompson, I. B., *La France. Population, Economie et Régions*, Doin Editeurs, Paris 1973, pp. 186-95.

5. Beaujeu-Garnier, J., 'Toward a new equilibrium in France', *Annals of the Association of American Geographers*, Vol. 64, No. 1, 1974, pp. 121-3.

6. Thompson, I. B., *The Paris Basin*, Oxford University Press, 1973.

7. Thompson, I. B., *The Lower Rhône and Marseille*, Oxford University Press, 1974.

8. Thompson, I. B., *Corsica*, David and Charles, 1971, pp. 98-103.

List of Contributors

JOHN B. AYTON, B.A., Dip.T.P., M.R.T.P.I., *Principal Planner, Planning Department, Norfolk County Council.*

R. A. BIRD, B.A., M.R.T.P.I., *Department of the Environment, formerly Director of the East Anglia Regional Strategy Team.*

P. J. DRUDY, M.Econ.Sc., M.A., Ph.D., *Lecturer, Department of Land Economy, University of Cambridge.*

D. P. GARBETT-EDWARDS, F.C.I.S., *Chief Executive, Mid-Wales Development Corporation, Newtown.*

DAVID KEEBLE, M.A., Ph.D., *Lecturer, Department of Geography, University of Cambridge.*

MALCOLM J. MOSELEY, M.Sc.(Econ.), M.A., Ph.D., *Lecturer, School of Environmental Science, University of East Anglia.*

D. C. NICHOLLS, M.A., Ph.D., *Lecturer, Department of Land Economy, University of Cambridge.*

IAN B. THOMPSON, M.A., Ph.D., *Professor, Department of Geography, University of Glasgow.*